Deromanticizing Black History

Critical Essays and Reappraisals

Clarence E. Walker

The University of Tennessee Press

KNOXVILLE

The paper in this book meets the minimum requirements
of the American National Standard for Permanence
of Paper for Printed Library Materials.
∞
The binding materials have been chosen
for strength and durability.

Library of Congress Cataloging in Publication Data

Walker, Clarence Earl.
    Deromanticizing Black history : critical essays and
reappraisals /
  Clarence E. Walker — 1st ed.
      p.   cm.
    Includes bibliographical references (p.   ) and index.
    ISBN 0-87049-721-9 (cloth : alk. paper)
    ISBN 0-87049-722-7 (pbk. : alk. paper)
    1. Afro-Americans — Historiography.   2. Southern States-
-Historiography.   I. Title.
    E184.65.W35   1991
    973′.0496073 — dc20   91-11073
                                              CIP

for
Henry Abelove
Erness Brody
Nathan Brody
Kate Gilbert
Marylin Katz
Robert O'Meally
Joseph Reed
Kit Reed
Rosalind Rosenberg
Richard Slotkin
Jerry Watts
Stephen White
Ann Wightman
Janice Willis
in affection and admiration

Contents

Acknowledgments

Writing and researching is a lonely business and in the process of preparing this manuscript for publication I have incurred a number of intellectual debts. I would like to thank the Wesleyan University Faculty Research Fund, the Meigs Fund of the Wesleyan University History Department, the Faculty Research Grants of the University of California, Davis, and the committee that awarded me a University of California President's Research Fellowship in the Humanities for the Academic Year 1989-1990. A special debt of thanks is owed to some of my former Wesleyan colleagues. Professors Andrew Barshay, Stewart Gillmore, Harris Friedberg, Patricia Hill, Oliver Holmes Jr., Bruce Masters, Donald Meyer, Ronald Schatz, Vera Schwarcz, and Richard Vann have read and criticized the manuscript at various stages of its preparation; the study has benefited greatly from their comments. I should also like to thank Donna Scott for typing numerous drafts of the first four chapters. Steven Lebergott, the interlibrary loan librarian of Wesleyan University, did a wonderful job of running down a number of obscure articles and titles. Thanks, Steven.

The University of California, Davis, is a wonderful place to work. I would like to thank David Brody, Dan Calhoun, Paul Goodman, Eugene Lunn, Ted Margadant, Barbara Metcalf, Ruth Rosen, Jeff Ruda, Vicki Ruiz, Michael Smith, Wilson Smith, and David Van Leer, all of whom read chapter one and suggested various emendations. A special thanks is owed Morton Rothstein, who has been both a colleague and teacher. I have learned a great deal about the South and the writing of history from Morton. He is a wonderful person. Robert Davidoff also gets a special word of thanks for his encouragement and criticism of my work. This book would not have been completed without the aid of Lynnda Borelli, James Brooks, Andrew Crowley, Jeff Ellis, Karen Hairfield, Cliff Hawkins, Jeff Kolnick, Kevin Leonard, Alan LoFaso, Nikki Mandell, Eric Martin, Salwa Nacuzzi, Chris Padgett, Jeff Reitzes, Joachim Roschmann, Jim Rose, Debbie Shields, Laura Simmons, L. Michael Smith, Melissa Vrana, and Jody Wall. As graduate students, typists, research assistants, and proofreaders these fine people have helped to bring this project to completion. Finally, in graduate school I met three characters who have enriched my intellectual and social life. We have been friends for over twenty years and I would like to thank Robert Abzug, Edmund Lee Drago, and Nick Salvatore. A number of the ideas explored in this manuscript were argued over either dinner, a drink, or the telephone. Thanks, guys.

Clarence E. Walker

Introduction

I have subtitled this book *Critical Essays and Reappraisals* because it is intended to fill a gap in the historiography of black Americans by looking critically at the problems of race, nationalism, slavery, and history. I am aware that my essays challenge some recent trends in the historiography of these subjects. They are to register my dissatisfaction with the (past and) current state of Afro-American history. Thirty years ago a new generation of historians brought a fresh perspective to the study of black people in America. I think it is now time to reconsider one of the major conceptual breakthroughs of that era in black history: the slave community/culturalist paradigm found in such well-known works as *The Slave Community, The Black Family in Slavery and Freedom, There is a River, From Sundown to Sunup, Slave Culture*, and *Deep Like the Rivers.*[1] All of these books are part of a historiographical revolution that began in the 1960s. They gave voice to a people who were thought to be silent, without historical agency, and thus merely ciphers in the history of the United States.

The history written in the sixties and seventies moved black people from the margins of the American past to center stage in the analysis of the country's political, social, and economic development. This history was a necessary corrective to an earlier mode of analysis that saw black people as passive victims of a past characterized by social pathology. "This model," as Nick Salvatore has recently written, "emphasized the weakness of the black family and stressed the effects of a high crime rate, broad under-employment, and the effect of single, female-headed family units upon Afro-American familial and community life"; the sources of this dysfunction lay in "the destructive effects of slavery and/or post-emancipation discrimination."[2] Within this tradition of analysis differing degrees of weight were accorded such factors as slavery, family disruption, crime, unemployment, and the hostility of white Americans to black people, but all of its proponents, including W.E.B. DuBois, E. Franklin Frazier, Kenneth B. Clark, Daniel Patrick Moynihan, Abram Kardiner, and Lionel Ovesey, saw the majority of black Americans as living in a world that was pathological and dysfunctional.[3] In the 1960s their line of argument fell into disrepute, as circumstances both internal and external to the historical profession reshaped our understanding of the American past in several ways.

First, the civil rights movement and the resurgence of nationalist sentiment among segments of the black community had a powerful impact on historians, both black and white.[4] Second, in the sixties, a new generation of historians began to ask different questions about the history of the United States. The effort to write history from the "bottom up" broadened the focus of historical inquiry and rendered visible groups heretofore invisible in the nation's past. Blacks, Indians, laborers, women, and members of other marginalized groups replaced the wealthy and the politically powerful as the central concern of American historians.[5] The idea that the Negro had emerged from slavery deracinated was abandoned and replaced by a paradigm which emphasized that, as slaves and free people, blacks drew on a rich repository of social and cultural sources to sustain them, their families, and their communities during their travail in America.[6] These new studies of black life in slavery and afterward gave culture a power and determinative force that I see no *prima facie* reason for allowing. John Blassingame, for example, emphasized the overriding force of black culture in his path-breaking analysis of the master-slave relationship: "The social organization of the quarters was the slave's primary environment, which gave him his ethical rules and fostered cooperation, mutual assistance, and black solidarity. The work experiences which most often brought the slave in contact with whites represented his secondary environment and was far less important in determining his personality than the primary environment."[7] Writing at the same time as Blassingame, George Rawick observed of slavery: ". . . while from sunup to sundown the American slave worked for another and was harshly exploited, from sundown to sunup he lived for himself and created the behavioral and institutional basis which prevented him from becoming the absolute victim."[8] This line of argument receives its most fulsome expression in Thomas Webber's discussion of slave education:

> Thus, to understand the nature of education in the slave quarter community is to come to grips with the paradox of the "free slave." Though the chains with which whites controlled black bodies were very real, try as they might, whites could not control black minds. These were molded from birth in an educational process created and managed by the quarter community. By passing their unique set of cultural themes from generation to generation, the members of the quarter community were able to resist most of white teaching, set themselves apart from white society, and molded their own cultural norms and group identity. While still legally slaves, the black men, women, and children of the quarter community successfully protected their psychological freedom and celebrated their human dignity.[9]

Blassingame, Rawick, and Webber bifurcate slave life. They separate work in the fields from life in the quarters. In their view, when slaves (male and female) entered the quarters and joined their family and friends, the concerns and problems that governed their workplace evaporated or disappeared. This is an improbable line of argument. Since 1956, when Kenneth Stampp published *The Peculiar Institution*, students of slavery have had a record of how alienating the work performed by slaves was. The destruction of work implements, malingering, and self-mutilation indicate an alienated work force.[10] Although no dominated population is ever completely socialized by its oppressors, the depictions found in slave community/culturalist studies of black life under bondage and afterward exaggerate the domestic autonomy and psychic health of the people being studied. "We simply cannot," as Bertram Wyatt-Brown has recently written, "continue expatiating on the riches of black culture without examining the social and psychological tensions that slavery entailed."[11] I am not suggesting a return to the pre-1956 interpretation of slavery. Rather, what is needed is a "more plausible" history of slavery and emancipation, one that pays close attention to both the strengths and weaknesses of black people in bondage.[12]

In counteracting the idea that slave culture was pathological, recent scholarship has tended to ignore the impact of powerlessness on the bondservant. Herbert Gutman overstated the case for the psychological autonomy of slaves when he wrote that ". . . slave belief had its origins within a cumulative slave experience."[13] The confidence and sense of self Gutman saw in a ". . . viable . . . culture with its own standards of behavior" was not something perceived by W.E.B. DuBois, writing nearly three-quarters of a century closer to the time of slavery.[14] According to DuBois slavery had produced a ". . . painful self-consciousness, an almost morbid sense of personality and a moral hesitancy which was fatal to self-confidence."[15] Undoubtedly the slave community had its own mores, but in the eyes of the slaves themselves these did not take precedence over those of the masters in the way that Gutman and the other proponents of the slave community/culturalist paradigm have argued. "The nigger during slavery was like sheep," a slave remarked. "We have always had to follow the white folks and do what we saw them do."[16] Commenting on slavery and mental health, Aby B. Jones, an escaped slave living in Canada, said "I believe it injurious to the mind of man. . . ."[17] Even as a free man, Frederick Douglass continued to feel the "moral hesitancy" which DuBois described as being fatal to "self-confidence." Called upon to speak at an abolitionist meeting, Douglass said, "I felt myself a slave."[18] William Wells Brown expressed a similar apprehensiveness after his escape from bondage. "I had never had a white man to treat me as an equal, and the idea of a white lady waiting on me at the table was still worse. Though the table was loaded with the good things of this life, I could not eat. I thought if I could only be allowed the privilege of eating in the kitchen, I should be more than satisfied!"[19] Such responses indicate the need to revise the idea that the slave community produced self-confident individuals who drew on an autonomous system of cultural resources.[20] This revision, it is to be hoped, will lead to a better understanding of the slave community and how it functioned.

A good place to begin this reevaluation is with the word "community." As the word is currently used by American historians in general, and students of black history in particular, the term is a romantic construct that obscures more than it reveals and posits community as an unproblematic *summum bonum* or *summum historicum*. Used in this way, it has "conjured up images," as Ellen McEwen has written in another context, "of harmony and cooperation, and brought to life feelings of personal responsibility, mutual aid and local initiative." In emphasizing these positive images, American historians have ignored "some of the nastier features of the close knit traditional 'communities' they idealized — their rigid inequalities, their intolerance and blood feuds."[21] True, by focusing on the blues, folk tales, ghost stories, the family, and religion, historians of slavery and emancipation have usefully elucidated a cultural system that served as the basis for a sense of peoplehood among black Americans. But this picture is too rosy and ignores such things as child abuse, racial self-hatred, and color prejudice. For example, the following entry (May 29, 1870) taken from Laura M. Towne's diary presents a very different picture of black family and child-rearing practices from that provided by Herbert Gutman. "The poor child," Towne noted of one of her students, "has been undergoing all sorts of ill treatment all winter from her father. She is a dwarf already, and he starved and beat her every day. She is one of the best scholars in my class, . . . but, under her father's management and direction, just as smart at lying and stealing. She often ran away to escape a beating, . . ."[22] How did the freed slave community handle this sort of parental behavior? Where were this slave child's benevolent kin?

In dealing with black people historians must get beyond the romantic notion that oppression produced a class of people who were inevitably kind and generous to their peers. The falseness of this notion can be seen most clearly in the racial self-hatred and oppositions based on color that have historically divided black America. None of the slave community/culturalist studies has dealt with these problems, despite their profound impact on the evolution of black American society in the nineteenth and twentieth centuries. Sarah Chase, a white teacher working with freed slaves in Savannah, Georgia, reprimanded an "old cotton picking 'auntie' for calling her fellows niggers."

> We are niggers," she said. "We always was niggers, and we always shall be; nigger here, and nigger there, nigger do this, and nigger do that. We've got no souls, we are animals. We are black and so is the evil one." "That you don't know," said S. "Yes I do," she replied. "The Bible does not say the devil is black," said S. "Well, white folks say so, and we'se bound to believe 'em, cause we'se nothing but animals and niggers. Yes, we'se niggers! niggers! niggers!"[23]

Although this example is an extreme instance of racial self-hatred, the black preacher-politician Henry M. Turner encountered a related problem in Georgia when trying to organize black people for the Republican party. "[We] want representative men, without regard to color, as long as they carry the brand of Negro oppression. . . . It does not matter whether he be a pretty or ugly Negro; a black Negro or a mulatto. . . . If he be, let him go to work, be his personal appearance as deformed as a jackass, or as charming as Venus."[24] Turner's frustration in trying to unite the black community was clearly not an isolated incident. In South Carolina a mulatto attending that state's 1868 constitutional convention remarked: "If ever there is a nigger government — an unmixed nigger government — established in South Carolina, I shall move."[25] A black delegate was equally uncharitable in his assessment of mulattoes. "To what race do they belong? . . . I know that my ancestors trod the burning sands of Africa, but why should men in whose veins run a greater preponderance of white blood seek to specially ally themselves with the black man, prate of 'our race,' when they are simply mongrels."[26] Racial self-hatred and color prejudice are only two of the problems that divided blacks before and after emancipation. In ignoring these divisions American historians have postulated a sense of community among blacks that never was: "community" generated by oppression is no true community. Community formed in response to oppression does not automatically become the constructive community these historians assume.[27]

This romanticizing of the slave and free communities can also be seen in Herbert Gutman's discussion of the black community's tolerant attitude toward pre-marital sex and illegitimacy. Gutman's work constitutes an important corrective to the work of E. Franklin Frazier and Daniel Patrick Moynihan.[28] Yet it has problems in its analysis of black sexuality. Gutman's argument is a complex one, but stripped of its complexity it underplays the impact of both African and Victorian morality on the slaves' culture and on the lives of the freed slaves. The African slaves brought to America in the seventeenth and eighteenth centuries came from cultures that disapproved of both pre-marital sex and illegitimacy. How is it that these slaves lost this sensibility and yet maintained such a strong sense of family and kinship in slavery? I do not think this happened to the degree that Gutman argues it did, The slave girl Linda Brent felt great shame when she had to tell her grandmother she was pregnant by a white man.[29] Commenting on her life after slavery, Sara Fitzpatrick observed, "Co'se I knows I ain't lived zackly right but I couldn't make dem men marry me."[30] Sara was the mother of several illegitimate children whom she loved dearly. The fact that none of the men she cohabited with married her seems to have troubled her. The lives of Linda Brent, Sara Fitzpatrick, and Margaret Lawrence all suggest that Gutman's analysis of black sexual attitudes needs to be rethought. Indeed, the recent fiction of black women writers indicates that these artists have a different perspective on the loose sexuality and informal community that Gutman sees as positive.[31] Historically, black literature has captured a number of the "realities of black alienation." as Bertram Wyatt-Brown has written, and historians writing about the black community should take some cues from this work.[32]

In calling for a re-examination of the slave community/culturalist paradigm, I want black history to rise above the romantic and celebratory.[33] Work that lacks these qualities has been dismissed or denounced as racist, reactionary, or examples of "thinking white."[34] This scholarly stance correlates intellectual acuity with racial authenticity. White scholars who adhere to this "party line" receive praise for "thinking black." For example, Nell Painter falls into this trap when she writes that "Lawrence Levine and Herbert Gutman, for instance, are able to think about history in what I'd call 'black ways.'"[35] Painter's appropriation of these two prominent white historians is nothing more than a procrustean exercise. What are "black ways" for thinking about history? Painter should heed the advice of a nineteenth-century black editor who once remarked: "The mind does not take its complexion from the skin."[36] Neither should the writing of history.

Put in a broader context, the romanticism that currently characterizes the writing of black history is really part of a problem inherent in the new social history. In their efforts to recreate a world we have lost, social historians have shed light on groups that were previously thought to be without history. But in accomplishing this goal they appear reluctant to apply the same standards of critical evaluation to "the people" that they apply to elites. The behavior of elites, as Jackson Lears has written, is often depicted as "mistaken, inappropriate, even perverse or irrational."[37] To make similar judgments about "the people" would be considered impolitic, elitist, or reactionary. This problem can be seen in recent work in both labor and southern history which has class conflict as its central focus.

Charles Beard's *An Economic Interpretation of the Constitution of the United States* gave class analysis a bad name in American history.[38] Beard's work aroused opposition because it ran counter to the idea that American society was a harmonious whole which had no social and economic divisions. But beginning in the 1950s class analysis became more respectable, and since the 1960s it has become commonplace in both labor and southern history.[39] Drawing inspiration and conceptualizations from E.P. Thompson's magisterial *The Making of the English Working Class* social historians have given voice to groups that a previous generation of American historians ignored.[40]

Following Thompson, these historians have used England as an "ideal-typical example of socio-economic transformation" for the nineteenth century.[41] But using a model based on the historical experience of the English working class, I would argue, is problematic. The class strife that disrupted English society in the nineteenth century was not replicated in the United States. American workers failed to develop a "working-class consciousness" and "culture" similar to that depicted in Thompson's study of class formation in England.[42] No historian of American labor or the South can say of northern workers and southern non-slaveholders what Eric Hobsbawm has observed of the "class consciousness" of British workers: "The lives of British workers were so impregnated with it that almost every one of their actions testified to their sense of difference and conflict between 'us' and 'them.'"[43] In a variety of ways the American worker failed to develop sensibilities independent of what British workers called "them."[44] This can be seen most clearly in the area of race in nineteenth-century ante- and postbellum America. Whites, whether they were rich or poor or lived in the North or South, considered black people their cultural, social, and political inferiors. Class analysis obscures this fact of American history "because in our national experience race has always been of greater importance than class."[45] In the United States, blacks traditionally have been objectified beyond their class position. This point has been either ignored or forgotten in the new social history.[46] Furthermore, when race has been included in this work it has been treated as a dependent variable and not accorded the relative autonomy it deserves. Race in the nineteenth century ought not to be conflated with class, as studies in labor and southern history have done recently. Treating "race as class" is an ahistorical formulation. Race in the nineteenth century was an autonomous historical phenomenon and occupied an analytical space of its own. Marxist and neo-Marxist techniques of folding or incorporating racial dynamics into economic dynamics risk minimizing the autonomy of racial conflict in the United States. As Eugene D. Genovese has written, ". . . American Marxists, as well as Americans generally, have greatly underestimated the depth of American racism, failing to understand its roots in a long historical past, and have therefore underestimated the difficulty of destroying racist attitudes and institutions."[47] To read some of the new social history a person would think that there were no ideas about race or racism in America before the rise of capitalism. Genovese clarifies the point thus: "Nor is the relation between capitalism and racism as clear and direct as many leftist critics assume. For one thing, the American North, like the South itself, was racist before its capitalism matured."[48]

Genovese confronts directly one of the deep conundrums of nineteenth-century United States history, namely, the question of why the white working class was so hostile to black people. "Labor in white skin," Karl Marx wrote in 1866, "cannot emancipate itself where the black skin is branded."[49] The answer to this question cannot be found in an analysis focusing on class consciousness. In the ante- and postbellum United States, people were divided along sectional, ethnic, gender, and religious lines. "Working-class consciousness, however inevitable and essential," Eric Hobsbawm has observed, "is probably politically secondary to other kinds of consciousness. As we know, where it has come into conflict in our century with national, or religious, or racial consciousness, it has usually yielded and retreated."[50] This was the case both before and after the Civil War in the United States. White labor in the North and South was Negrophobic. For the new social history to rise above the romantic and celebratory in its explication of our nation's past, it must confront what has heretofore been "impolitic": the racism of the white working class in the nineteenth century.[51] How did working-class antipathy to blacks slow the process of democratization and opportunity in American society? This animus cannot be explained away as a product either of capitalist manipulation or false consciousness.

The answer to this problem lies in an analysis of working-class attitudes that focuses on something other than the mode of production. The first essay in this collection has such a focus. I call this piece "How Many Niggers Did Karl Marx Know? or, A Peculiarity of the Americans," even though both colleagues and critics have objected to this title. Both parties have taken exception to my use of the epithet "nigger," though for different reasons. I chose the title because it was ironic and shocked people. In doing so, I was aware that Marx's philosophy of history did "not account," as Shlomo Avineri has observed, "for the majority of mankind since it was relevant only to the European experience."[52] The epithet also seemed appropriate because it emphasizes the extent to which historically in America black people have been objectified beyond their class position. The word "nigger" was and is a crucial component in this process of objectification. During the nineteenth century all black people, rich or poor, slave or free, were "niggers." Courtesies accorded whites because of their class position were denied Negroes with similar accomplishments in ante- and postbellum America.[53] In this practice the United States was unique among New World slave societies both before and after emancipation.[54]

Marxist and neo-Marxist readers will accuse me of according race a "transhistorical" or "metaphysical" place in my analysis of nineteenth-century American society, suggesting that I have not paid close attention to context.[55] According to this line of argument the social world of the nineteenth century changed, as did ideas about race and racism. I agree that the social world changed over the course of the nineteenth century, but I do not think there was a corresponding change in American racial attitudes, at least not to the degree that my critics want to argue or believe. The Civil War and Reconstruction constitute, for example, major turning points in American history. But these two events did not transform American race relations. The slaves were free but their freedom was different from that of other free people. Emancipation did not eradicate the idea that Negroes were different from whites. In the analysis of a social system too much weight can be placed

on political, social, and economic change, as recent work in southern history has done.[56] What this scholarship assumes is that the
South in particular, and the United States generally, experienced
a break and reformation of their racial sensibilities because of
war and conflict. This assumption is naive, for no society is ever
completely transformed by upheaval.[57] If we broaden our perspective this point becomes clear.

Thus, for example, French Jews were emancipated during the
era of the French Revolution. But although the Revolution transformed European society in many ways in the eighteenth and nineteenth centuries, anti-Semitism continued to plague not only
French Jews but European Jews generally.[58] To be sure the social
world these people lived in changed, but there was still anti-
Semitism in that world. In a similar way, American Negroes, although free after the Civil War and Reconstruction, continued to
be treated as though they were racially inferior to whites. Closer
to our own times, the revolution in Russia did not end anti-
Semitism there. And in China a similar transformation has not
eradicated deeply ingrained beliefs that female children are less
valuable than male children. Nor did the Chinese revolution re-
move a historic hostility to black people, as recent events indicate.[59]

Both China and Japan are societies in which there are no in-
digenous black people and in which, until the colonial era, there
has been no contact with blacks. Nevertheless, both countries' antipathy to blacks is deeply embedded. This hostility cannot be explained in terms of market forces or modes of production. In
Japan, Hiroshi Wagatsuma has written, "Long before any sustained contact with either Caucasoid Europeans or dark-skinned
Africans or Indians, the Japanese valued 'white' skin as beautiful
and deprecated 'black' skin as ugly." Historically, Wagatsuma continues, "the Japanese have always associated skin color symboli-
cally with other physical characteristics that signify degrees of
spiritual refinement or primitiveness."[60] How different is this from
the western association of blackness with evil and sensuality?
Returning to Japan in 1860, after his boat stopped on the African
coast, a Japanese envoy wrote "The black ones look like devils

depicted in pictures. The faces are black as if painted with ink and their physiognomy reminds me of that of a monkey."[61] These Japanese perceptions of black people duplicate those of nineteenth-century whites, for both groups saw Negroes as "primitive, childish simple-minded natives."[62]

The Japanese example also provides an interesting test case for the proponents of class analysis, particularly with respect to their claim that the language of race and class are the same.[63] In Japan there is a group of people called the Eta. According to the Japanese, the "Eta, as they are termed, are descendants of a less human 'race' than the stock that fathered the Japanese nation as a whole." In Japan the Eta "bear the same social stigma as that borne by the American Negro." Prior to their emancipation in 1871 the Eta were "visibly distinguishable by the special garb they were forced to wear and by other social attributes that prevented them from becoming invisible." Today this "pariah caste is completely indistinguishable in any sense from the population as a whole, whose segregation nevertheless has long been justified in racial terms."[64] Discrimination against the Eta in Japan, like discrimination against blacks in nineteenth-century America, was rooted in "deep seated fears of racial contamination and loss of purity as a result of possible interbreeding."[65] In both cultures the outgroup was treated as a pathogen. Thus when the Japanese called the Eta "four legged" they were making a comment about race, not class, two categories which my first essay is intended to establish as distinctly separate.[66]

Marcus Garvey has been accorded a privileged position in American historiography, and accordingly, to criticize Garvey or his movement is neither fashionable nor politically correct.[67] In my second essay I attempt to make the discussion of Garvey something more than an exercise in hagiography. The recent work of Wilson J. Moses and Judith Stein also represents a departure from the celebratory tradition. But Stein's preoccupation with class blinds her to the racist appeal of Garvey's movement.[68] Lawrence W. Levine's essay in *Black Leaders of the Twentieth Century* is interesting but fails to come to grips with the unpleasant side of Garveyism.[69] The Levine essay is also unclear in its general claim that Garvey revitalized black American culture. In his splendid book *Black Culture and Black Consciousness* Levine analyzed black American folk culture with insight and sensitivity. However, his essay fails to note that Garvey had no appreciation of folk culture, whether that of black Americans or Jamaican peasants; his standard of civilization was the aristocratic culture of the British Empire, not the blues of Bessie Smith.[70] I also think that Levine's statement that Garvey's black American followers thought their "blackness was nothing to apologize for; that black men and women shared a common proud heritage" needs to be revised.[71] Garvey's arrival in the United States coincided with the work of Carter G. Woodson and The Association for the Study of Negro Life and History. This organization was founded to correct an idea shared by both black and white Americans that Negroes living in the United States had no history. How did Garvey then revitalize the historical consciousness of American blacks?[72] If Garvey did revive a long-dormant sense of pride among black Americans, was this unproblematic? How did Garveyism, for example, affect black political activity in the cities of the North and South in the 1920s?

The distinguished black man of letters J. Saunders Redding provides an answer to these questions in his book *On Being Negro in America*.[73] Redding grew up in Wilmington, Delaware. In this city, before the arrival of the Garveyites, Negroes living in one political ward "had no trouble electing one of their own to the school board and another to the city council. The same men had been returned to office time and again. What they did there (and they did little) seemed not nearly so important as just being there. They had enormous prestige and influence among Negroes, and they had not had to fight to keep it." This situation changed when Garvey's followers "put up their own candidates, chosen on class lines: the incumbents who, in the common phrase, were 'dickties' found their following split." The end result was disaster for the "dickties": they were outsmarted by the Garveyites, who "made a deal with the white leaders in the ward."[74] Although this is only one incident it points to the problem of casting Garvey's movement in the Whig model of history. What this example indicates instead is that Garvey's calls for racial unity were self-serving, empty slogans. People who disagreed with Garvey's program were branded traitors to the race. But were these people committing treason or merely asserting their right not to be coerced by something they found questionable?

Some will note that I have not relied on Professor Robert Hill's editions of the Garvey papers, which were in the process of being published when I wrote my essay. Although I have read in the Hill edition of the Garvey papers as they have appeared and also reviewed volume 4 of the Garvey papers for *The New York Times* on December 22, 1985, nothing that I have read in them after completing my essay has caused me to change the main line of my argument. I still think Garveyism was racist and reactionary, an assertion not of black American culture but of the culture of black British West Indians transposed to the United States. I happen to think that Garvey was a charlatan who diverted American blacks from the racial struggle in the United States. The essay, in short, is critical of Garvey. It also raises questions about the choices black people have made in the past. Black people in the New Social History occupy a sacrosanct position; their actions cannot be queried. This intellectual position denies black people the freedom to be wrong.

This view has provoked widespread opposition from both the audiences to whom I have presented this essay and the journals in which I have tried to have it published. The response from one Canadian referee in particular is noteworthy because it illustrates the dangerous habit of correlating intellectual acuity with racial authenticity: "There are two views about Garvey in the U.S.A., one held by Black people and one held by white Americans. They do not agree, of course. His discussion is on the side of the latter."[5]

My essay on Eugene D. Genovese's *Roll, Jordan, Roll* was also deemed politically incorrect and was difficult to get published. What I said about this book in 1980 has now become mainstream. My essay differs in one respect, however, from most of the criticism made of *Roll, Jordan, Roll*. I found Professor Genovese's explication of slave religion puzzling.[76] Having grown up with two black, church-attending grandmothers born in the nineteenth century, I found that Genovese's functional account of the religion of American slaves corresponds in no way to what I was taught by my grandmothers. Anyone who has been in the black church knows the centrality of the doctrine of original sin and the importance of Jesus in black Christianity. I do not think Genovese's analysis of the religion of American slaves pays adequate attention to either of these aspects of black faith.

Finally, the essay on W.E.B. DuBois's *Black Reconstruction* and the article on the writing of black history from 1836 to 1935 are preliminary findings of a current research project. This project will trace the writing of black history by both black and white historians from 1836 to 1986.

These essays are all presented as they were originally written in the mid to late 1980s. Any duplication from one to another stems from the fact that each essay was written as a self-contained piece of work rather than as a chapter of a book. What unites this collection is the principle of revisionism. The issues addressed in these essays, as this introduction has indicated, have drawn sharp reactions from those who have read or listened to my presentation of them. This is what good historical work should do. I hope this little book will stimulate further work and a reevaluation of the field.

Deromanticizing Black History

How Many Niggers Did Karl Marx Know?
Or, A Peculiarity of the Americans

This essay is about black and white people in nineteenth-century America. It argues that race, not class, was the primary division in American society under slavery before the Civil War. Race remained the primary division after the war in a segregated society. In taking this position I want to raise questions about the kind of class analysis currently employed by some Americans who study southern history.[1] Although the work of these scholars has raised new questions that are both provocative and interesting, race is no longer at the center of studies of pre- and postwar southern society. Influenced by Progressive, Marxist, and neo-Marxist paradigms of history that emphasize class conflict, Barbara Fields, Steven Hahn, Armistead Robinson, and Jonathan Wiener have created a nineteenth century where race and racial antipathy have been relegated to the periphery of the national consciousness. Two examples drawn from studies of politics and community in ante- and postbellum Georgia illustrate this point. "Whatever the differing milieu of slavery on farms and whatever the force of racism in its own right," Steven Hahn has written, "the attitudes of the yeomanry toward Afro-Americans must be understood, historically, as attitudes of petty property owners toward the property-less poor — attitudes which at certain junctures led smallholders to join with the upperclass in defining the dispossessed out of the political community."[2] What is Hahn saying here? Is he saying that blacks were excluded from Georgia's antebellum political community because they lacked property? If so, why were propertied free Negroes denied the franchise? Armistead Robinson pursues a similar line of argument in his article "Beyond the Realm of Social Consensus: New Meanings of Reconstruction for American History." In this essay Robinson dances around the issue of race in Reconstruction politics in Georgia.

> What is clear, however, is that the fatal splits within the Georgia biracial coalition emerged first over economic issues and only subsequently over questions of race equality. The heavy contribution racial tensions made to the final demise of Georgia Republicanism is beyond doubt. But the party's leaders recognized from the outset that their party would govern only as long as Republicans sustained white support. It was the effort to harness two antagonistic white social classes that prompted the critical initial slippage among white voters. Racial hostilities became an increasingly important factor, but they did not give rise to the basic cleavages within the Georgia Republican party. Rather, racial tension administered the coup de grace to an already mortally wounded organization.[3]

This is interesting analysis, but it does not reflect the racial reality that was at the heart of Georgia Republicanism. In Georgia the Republican party had 120,000 members in 1869. Blacks outnumbered whites in the party ranks by a ratio of three to one. Racial division not class antagonisms destroyed the Republican Party in Georgia.[4] Robinson is wrong, therefore, when he writes "Racism did not overwhelm class; racism became an organizing principle for social strata fearful of class-based political action."[5]

Together Hahn and Robinson exemplify the neo-Marxist penchant for treating racial tension as a by-product of economic struggles. In short, for them race has no independent status of its own as a variable. Concerned with capturing a world we have lost this new history criticizes capitalism because it destroyed a supposedly cozy communal past. Just what role race and racism played in the lives of the people inhabiting this golden age is unclear. This mode of analysis submerges racial oppression in a larger construct of class antipathies. Race is swept under the carpet of class analysis and becomes a dependent variable in the historic clash of classes "over power and privilege; over oppression and exploitation, over competing senses of justice and right."[6] The notion of class as a conceptual and interpretive tool denies important distinctions that existed in the treatment accorded poor whites and blacks in the South,[7] distinctions illustrated by the words of a sharecropper, Nate Shaw:

> If a white man moved on Aker's land he was liable to stay for many years, and his children too, if there was land enough for them to work. Some of them that started with nothin' has become wealthy. But all the niggers caught the devil down there. Wiped out the niggers and gived the benefit of the land to the whites.[8]

A class analysis also makes invisible the unique struggle of black people for freedom and equality in nineteenth-century America. The black quest for equality had its own autonomy, which grew out of the peculiar circumstances of black life in ante- and postbellum America.[9]

In the nineteenth century, black people, whether slave or free, were forced because of their color and physiognomy to relate to white people in ways that set them apart from other groups in America society. As Robert Blauner has observed:

> Racist social relations have different cultural consequences from class relations and therefore . . . cannot be forced into the procrustean bed of lower-class culture. . . . Racism excludes a category of people from participation in society in a different way than does class hegemony and exploitation. The thrust of racism is to dehumanize, to violate dignity and degrade personalities in a much more pervasive and all-inclusive way than class exploitation — which in the United States, at any rate, has typically not been generalized beyond the point of production. For these reasons, racial and class oppression — while intimately interacting — have diverse consequences for group formation, for the salience of identities based upon them, and for individual and group modes of adaptation and resistance.[10]

Blauner's distinction between race- and class-based social relations is substantiated by Nate Shaw. Speaking of his relations with his white boss, Shaw says:

> It's stamped in me in my mind, the way I have been treated, the way
> I have seed other colored people treated — couldn't never go by what
> you think or say, had to come up to the white man's orders. "You
> ain't got sense enough to know this; you ain't got sense enough to
> know that, you ain't got sense enough to know nothin — just let me
> tell you how to do what I want you to do." Well, that's disrecogniz-
> ing me . . . Just disrecognized, discounted in every walk of
> life. . . . [11]

In the nineteenth century, social interaction between blacks
and whites proceeded on the principle of "disrecognizing." Black
people were objectified beyond their class position. An analysis
of nineteenth-century black history, therefore, that focuses solely
on the Negroes' relationship to the mode of production obscures
more than it reveals. Regardless of their accomplishments, Negroes
did not climb the ladder of American social mobility as whites
did. Successful Negroes did not redeem the race as a whole or indicate their people's potential for making it in nineteenth-century
American society.[12] No matter what they achieved, they were still,
in the parlance of the day, "only niggers."[13] As David Potter has
written:

> The purpose of history is not simply to show that events which
> might have happened to anyone did happen to someone, but rather
> to explain why a special sequence of events befell a particular ag-
> gregation of people. To do this, history must find, as a unifying fac-
> tor, what is distinctive in the circumstances, the condition, the ex-
> perience of the aggregation in question.[14]

The unifying factor in the aggregate experience of nineteenth-
century Americans was race, not class. Thus, the history of the
American Negro in the nineteenth century poses a problem for
Karl Marx's intellectual heirs.

Marx's historical sociology was primarily concerned with in-
terpreting the industrial order that had replaced feudalism. Ethnic
and racial conflicts were not subjects to which Marx gave much
close attention. Although Marx acknowledged these types of division in society, he does not appear to have been much interested
in explaining their dynamics.[15] Obsessed with a supposedly more

fundamental category of socioeconomic identity, namely class, Marx slighted race and did not grant it a place of its own in his historical work. In 1849, in response to the query "What is a Negro slave?" Marx wrote: "A man of the black race. The one explanation is as good as the other. . . . A Negro is a Negro."[16] To Thomas Jefferson, John C. Calhoun, William Lowndes Yancey, and Alexander Stephens, Marx's statement would have constituted what Ambrose Bierce called a "vagrant opinion, one without visible means of support."[17] In the eyes of these statesmen and the people they represented, Negroes were primitive, comical outsiders who were governed more by appetite than reason. That is, they had an essence – albeit a debased one – which Marx's tautology (a Negro is a Negro) did not apprehend. George Bancroft captured this aspect of nineteenth-century American thought when he wrote that black people were "gross and stupid, having memory and physical strength but . . . undisciplined in the exercise of reason and imagination."[18] Bancroft expressed in this observation a widely held belief, one that cut across class, ethnic, and sectional lines. To most nineteenth-century white Americans the Negroes' racial difference and inferiority were not mere abstractions. Race was a physical fact. To argue as one recent student of southern history has that for nineteenth-century whites race was a "purely ideological notion" is arrant, ahistorical nonsense.[19] Those American historians who have noted that racial antipathy was a major factor in the history of the United States have not been engaged in some sort of exceptionalism, as has sometimes been alleged.[20] Nor have they accorded "race a transhistorical, almost metaphysical, status that removes it from all possibility of analysis and understanding."[21] On the contrary, what scholars such as Carl Degler, George Fredrickson, Winthrop Jordan, Leon Litwack, Michael Rogin, Richard Slotkin, and Joel Williamson have done is to pay close attention to race and racial thinking, as it evolved in Euro-American thought.[22]

Beginning in the late 1890s Franz Boas and his associates began to question scientific and popular thinking about race. Boas's assault on race as a "supraindividual organic identity" lasted almost half a century, and it was not until the 1930s that the idea of race as some sort of biologically determined datum began to lose credence in American society. Before Boas, both before and after the creation of the United States, people thought that race was an observable physical fact.[23] In analyzing this problem historians have taken account of the political, social, economic, and psychological context within which American racism flourished. Focusing on this issue, they have dealt with a cultural peculiarity of American society, that is, the presence of large numbers of people of African descent. Negroes were not a problem in nineteenth-century metropolitan Europe, whose nations never fought bloody Civil Wars over the place of black people in their future.[24] Furthermore, the American working class, as Mike Davis has suggested, was different from its European counterpart.[25]

The white people who lived in ante- and postbellum America defined themselves in a variety of ways, by region, gender, religion, ethnicity, and race. Noting these differences cannot be dismissed as an exercise in exceptionalism.[26] Nor is the problem of American deviation from European patterns of class conflict solved by subsuming this issue under the currently fashionable umbrella of "republicanism."[27]

White American farmers and workers in the nineteenth century may have found in "republicanism" a counter-hegemonic ideology that protected them from the excesses of bourgeois liberalism.[28] "Republicanism," however, did not free these people of the racial antipathies that pervaded American society. Virtually all white Americans, rural and urban, agrarian and industrial laborers, agreed that the Negro was their social, cultural, and political inferior. This belief had a profound effect on American politics and culture both before and after the Civil War. W.E.B. DuBois, whose life bridged the nineteenth and twentieth centuries, understood this when he wrote of Marxism:

> This philosophy did not envisage a situation where instead of a
> horizontal division of classes, there was a vertical fissure, a complete
> separation of classes by race, cutting square across the economic
> layers. Even if on one side of this color line, the dark masses were

overwhelmingly workers, with but an embryonic capitalist class, nevertheless the split between white and black workers was greater than between white workers and capitalists; and this split depended not simply on economic exploitation but on a racial folk-lore grounded on centuries of instinct, habit and thought and implemented by the conditional reflex of visible color.[29]

In nineteenth-century America, this "racial folk-lore" undermined in an important way the actualization of Marx's paradigm of history.

In the nineteenth century there was no precise idea of what constituted race. Although there were a number of efforts to develop a taxonomy of mankind, these efforts produced more controversy than consensus.[30] Nevertheless, there was a conception of race implicit in the doctrine of permanent human types.[31] The prevailing notion among white Americans, both before and after the Civil War, was that black people were physically and mentally different from themselves and that, because they were dissimilar, the two groups could not live together in the same country as equals. President Lincoln expressed this idea on August 14, 1862, to a black delegation he had summoned to the White House. Pessimistic about the future of Negroes in the United States, Lincoln told the assembled blacks that "you and we are different races. We have between us a broader difference than exists between any other two races. Whether it is right or wrong I need not discuss, but this physical difference is a great disadvantage to us both, as I think your race suffer very greatly, many of them by living among us, while ours suffer from your presence. . . ."[32] In asserting that blacks and whites were physically different, Lincoln recapitulated an idea expressed by Thomas Jefferson in his *Notes on the State of Virginia*. "I advance it therefore, as a suspicion only," Jefferson wrote, "that the blacks, whether originally a distinct race, or made distinct by time and circumstances, are inferior to the whites in the endowments both of body and mind."[33] Jefferson's "suspicion" became, in the nineteenth century, an *idée fixe* of American popular culture. Defined as "different and inferior," black people occupied a marginal place in ante- and postbellum society. As social, political, and moral aliens they were in America but not of it.

By focusing on labor struggles, institutions like slavery, or periods of crisis such as Reconstruction and Populism, some historians have given class and class conflict a privileged position in nineteenth-century American history.[34] Within this framework of analysis, race is accorded a subordinate role, as an issue used in political disputes by elites to maintain their power.[35] But did the ante- and postbellum elite have to use race to maintain their power? Or was race a phenomenon with its own autonomy, something not dependent on the viscissitudes of the economy or political infighting between different groups of Caucasians? Race as a force in American history becomes clearer if we take what Fernand Braudel calls the "longue durée," a historical perspective of America that rises above "histoire évenementielle" or the history of events.[36] From the perspective of nineteenth-century black American history, race and racism had a force that transcended the squabbles of elite and non-elite whites over power and privilege. The persistence of this idea had to do with the belief that the Negro was physically and mentally different from whites. White black-faced minstrels expressed this sensibility when they sang the following lyrics:

> Niggers hair am berry short,
> White folks hair am longer,
> White folks dey smell very strong,
> Niggers dey smell stronger.[37]

Nineteenth-century American racism, like its European counterpart, had a strong aesthetic or visual component. Caucasian features, especially those that captured the lineaments of classical civilization, were highly prized.[38] The Negro's physiognomy did not correspond to this ideal type. Dr. Samuel Cartwright, for example, although conceding the Negroes' humanity, thought that black people were "anatomically constructed, about the head and face, more like the monkey tribes and the lower order of animals than any other species of the genus man." Negro men, while performing the dance called "patting juber," according to Dr. Cartwright, emitted an odor so powerful that it threw "negro women into paroxysms of unconciousness, *vulgo* hysterics."[39] Simply to dismiss Dr. Cartwright's observations as absurd and ridiculous would be a mistake. For in the nineteenth century, as the Reverend Hosea Easton observed, "the colored people subserved almost every foul purpose imaginable."[40] The words "Negro" and "nigger" had a host of negative connotations in the popular mind.

> Negro or nigger, is an approbrious term, employed to impose contempt upon them as an inferior race, and also to express their deformity of person. Nigger lips, nigger shins, and nigger heels are phrases universally common among the juvenile class of society, and full well understood by them; they are early learned to think of these expressions, as they are intended to apply to colored people, and as being expressive or descriptive of the odious qualities of their mind and body.[41]

Such characterizations had a profound effect on the young:

> The first lessons given are, Johnny, Billy, Mary, Sally, (or whatever the name may be,) go to sleep, if you don't the old nigger will care you off; don't you cry — Hark; the old niggers' coming — how ugly you are, you are worse than a little nigger. This is a specimen of the first lessons given.

> The second is generally given in the domestic circle; in some families it is almost the only method of correcting their children. To inspire their half grown misses and masters to improvement, they are told that if they do this or that or if they do thus and so, they will be poor or ignorant as a nigger; or that they will be black as a nigger; or have no more credit than a nigger; that they will have hair, lips, feet, or something of the kind, like a nigger. . . . See nigger's thick lips — see his flat nose — nigger eye shine — that slick looking nigger — nigger, where you get so much coat? — that's a nigger priest — are sounds emanating from little urchins of Christian villagers, which continually infest the feelings of colored travellers, like a pestiferous breath of young devils; and full grown persons, and sometimes professors of religion, are not unfrequently heard to join in the concert.[42]

These negative perceptions of black people were carried from childhood into adult life. Operating as a negative reference group,

Negroes told whites who they were and were not. If we take Braudel's "longue durée," we can see that throughout the nineteenth century black Americans were treated as though they were a pathogen. In the North, discrimination and segregation kept Negroes living on the margins of society and away from whites. South of the Mason and Dixon line, slavery and segregation served a similar function.[43]

Underlying the proscription and objectification of black people was a great fear of Negro men and women as sexual beings. The emphasis that white Americans placed on the Negro's physical appearance points to a deeply rooted fear of racial intermixture. Amalgamation, it was thought, would destroy Caucasians physically and mentally.[44] Josiah Priest expressed this fear when he wrote that the union of blacks and whites would result in a "universal retrograde from the moral image of God toward the condition of brutes." The "intellectuality of the white race would be destroyed from the earth," Priest asserted, "and merged in the thick skulls of the negroes."[45] And during the struggles over Kansas and Nebraska, in the 1850s, white girls paraded the streets of a midwestern town with banners reading: "Fathers, save us from nigger husbands."[46] Echoing this frame of mind, *The Argus Democrat* of Madison, Wisconsin, told its readers in 1857 that "whenever these lines of demarkation [*sic*] are endeavored to be obliterated by amalgamation, the white race has been degenerated, enfeebled, and degraded as a material consequence."[47] To prevent the unthinkable from occurring, laws against racial intermarriage were passed during the colonial period and after the creation of the democratic republic. What these ordinances symbolize, David Fowler has written, is "white fear of . . . change in the structure of white society as well as resistance to change of any kind in the system of subordination of non-whites."[48] This fear of amalgamation was born of hysteria stemming from rapid social change. Interracial marriage was extremely rare in the nineteenth century. Blacks and whites brave enough to embark on this perilous course were universally condemned, and the children produced by these unions were called an "abominable mixture."[49]

The hysteria which the presence of mulattoes evoked in American society must be placed in a broader context. If the Negro was a pathogen, what Mary Douglas has called "matter out of place,"[50] the mulatto was a still more extreme contradiction of the normal or natural order of things. The presence of mulattoes in American society, Winthrop Jordan has argued, presented "incontrovertible evidence that sheer animal sex was governing . . . American destiny and that the great experiment in the wilderness had failed to maintain the social and personal restraints which were the hallmarks and the very stuff of civilization."[51] Miscegenation represented a breakdown in the social distance between blacks and whites. This division was central to America's definition of itself as a white man's country. Whites who coupled with blacks were ". . . depraved persons who had given themselves up to a wicked perversion of the sexual instincts."[52] Coupling with the black beast was "either pruriently disgusting or obscenely exciting," Calvin Hernton has written.[53] For nineteenth-century white Americans the Negro penis and vagina were organs of both terror and pleasure. This can be seen in the mythology which Caucasians created about Negro sexuality: all black males were overly endowed, and Negro females possessed vaginas whose copulative strength made them legendary in the folklore of American sexuality.[54] In the South, slave women were Jezebels whose libidinousness posed a threat to the southern white family. According to one southern writer: "The heaviest part of the white racial burden in slavery was the African woman, of strong sex instincts and devoid of sexual conscience at the white man's door, in the white man's dwelling."[55]

The construction of this myth of sexuality tells us more about the whites who manufactured it than it does about the sexual mores and behavior of black people. For example, when southern white men described black women as being hot or sexually ardent they created a rationale for their own acts of infidelity: responsibility for the white man's lapses of morality was thereby shifted to the black woman.[56] Similarly, when white men claimed on the one hand that black men lusted after white women, and in the same breath described white women as passionless, they were being disingenuous.[57] If white women were so cold and frigid, then why did black men desire them? Was the essence of black male sexuality necrophilia? The answer is no. When white men desexualized their women, they were actually saying that these women were desirable. Because they were desirable, white women had to be protected from the lust of black beasts. Indeed, given the central role that white women played in southern thought and society, is it not possible to think of the South in some sense as a gynecocracy? Historians who regularly refer to the South as a patriarchy ignore the power which white women exercised in ante- and postbellum southern society. These women's power was not political, but it was cultural and biological.[58] As mothers and wives, southern white women were "custodians of culture."[59] They saw to it that the cultural values and beliefs of white southerners were passed from one generation to the next. In their reproductive capacity they produced children whose births guaranteed that the South would remain dominated by white Anglo-Saxon Protestants. In short, white women were central actors in that relationship which Cash has called the "Proto-Dorian convention."[60]

A discussion of white perceptions and fears about black sexuality is central to any understanding of American race relations before and after the Civil War. Although he was writing in the twentieth century, James Weldon Johnson understood this when he wrote "in the core of the heart of the American race problem the sex factor is rooted."[61] Johnson went on to say that the problem was so deeply rooted "that it is not always recognized when it shows at the surface. Other factors are obvious and are the ones we dare to deal with; but, regardless of how we deal with these, the race situation will continue to be acute as long as the sex factor persisted."[62] What Johnson called the "sex factor" has indeed persisted, as has the problem of race. In the nineteenth century, sex and sexuality were troubling issues for white Americans in both the North and South, and the presence of Negroes in the United States only added to their disquiet about the basic human drive.[63] The "sex act," as Winthrop Jordan has observed, "served as a ritualistic re-enactment of the daily pattern of white social dominance."[64]

I would argue that these anxieties about the place of blacks in American society took precedence over class conflict in the postwar South. But what of the treatment accorded northern free Negroes before the Civil War? Their history also confounds a class analysis and raises questions about its applicability to postwar southern society.[65] The North's treatment of its free Negro population prefigured the South's adoption of racial separation.[66] Segregation was not, as C. Vann Woodward has shown, essential to the maintenance of plantation slavery. Since urban life was the exception rather than the rule in the antebellum South, free blacks who resided in the larger cities of the slave states found their lives circumscribed by a "rudimentary pattern of segregation."[67] In the North the separation of the races was more systematic.[68] Economically, politically, and socially, the northern Negro was a pariah. "Race prejudice seems stronger in those states that have abolished slavery than in those where it still exists," Alexis de Tocqueville wrote in the 1830s, "and nowhere is it more intolerant than in those states where slavery was never known."[69] The testimony of a number of free persons of color corroborates de Tocqueville's observation. Charlotte Forten, the granddaughter of James Forten, a wealthy black Philadelphia sailmaker, wrote in her diary that some of her friends were refused admission to the "Museum, . . . solely on account of their complexion."[70] On another occasion Miss Forten recorded that she and a "Mrs. Putnam . . . were refused at two ice cream saloons, successively."[71] Charlotte Forten and her friends were educated, free Negroes, but their learning and other cultural attainments, rather than earning them respect, earned them contempt. *The Colored American*, February 23, 1839, commented on this strange state of affairs. "A colored man may be blessed with the highest and most cultivated intellect," the paper said, "may be clothed with all the Christian graces, yet as long as he is debarred from an equal participation in political privilege, he will be despised and trampled on by the majority in power."[72] In a society in which self-improvement was a highly prized value, Negroes who succeeded were nonetheless treated differently from their white peers. "The educated Negro in America is a greater sufferer than the uneducated," the Reverend Samuel Ringgold Ward asserted. "An educated Negro, as a rule, is treated no better than one undereducated . . . he is made the object of peculiarly offensive treatment, because of his superior attainments; he is said to be 'out of his place,' he is thought to be 'assuming the place of a white man.'"[73] Color, not class, bound the northern free Negro. Traveling in the United States on the eve of the Civil War, Edward W. Blyden remarked that "color was the sign of every insult and contumely."[74] Money did not whiten in North America as it did in some parts of Latin America.[75]

Indeed, one of the ironies of nineteenth-century black history is the great faith black people placed in embourgeoisement as the solution to their problems as outsiders. Both before and after the Civil War black spokesmen such as Frederick Douglass encouraged their people to become respectable and propertied. "Men are not valued in this country," Douglass wrote, "for what they are; they are valued for what they can do."[76] To overcome this disability Douglass encouraged his people to "get wisdom" and "get knowledge."[77] By pursuing "an honest, upright life," Douglass said, "we may at least wring from a reluctant public the all important confession, that we are men, worthy men, good citizens, good Christians, and ought to be treated as such."[78] Douglass was not alone in his belief that self-improvement would "wring" from white Americans the respect free northern Negroes desired. This belief was shared by William Wells Brown, Henry Highland Garnet, Martin R. Delaney, the Reverend Thomas McCants Stewart, and Hosea Easton, as Waldo Martin has shown.[79] These black men believed that their people's problems stemmed from their "condition," not their "color."[80] Improve the Negro's "condition" and color, black spokesmen thought, would become immaterial. In taking this stance Douglass and his peers rejected the white supremacist credo that a black skin was a badge of racial inferiority.

The efforts of free Negroes to improve themselves were fraught with difficulties, however. Black efforts at self-improvement were viewed with unease by the white population of the North. And although racial antipathy cut across class lines, it was most intense among the white laboring classes.[81] Writing in 1830 "A Colored Philadelphian" asserted "if a man of color has children, it is almost impossible for him to get a trade for them, as the journeymen and apprentices generally refuse to work with them, even if the master is willing, which is seldom the case."[82] Frederick Douglass, a black man who for the most part believed in the promise of American life, remarked in a pessimistic moment: "Prejudice against the free colored people in the United States has shown itself nowhere so invincible as among the mechanics. The farmer and the professional man cherish no feeling so bitter as that cherished by these. The latter would starve us out of the country entirely."[83] By 1853 things had become so bleak that Douglass could say that the "old avocations, by which colored men obtained a livelihood, are rapidly, increasingly and inevitably passing into other hands." These new hands belonged to immigrants whose "color," Douglass remarked, gave them title to the Negroes' jobs.[84]

Labor historians have seen the violence between free blacks and whites in terms of class conflict, but I think this is a mistake.[85] These conflicts were race wars. The intensity of the hatred that native whites and immigrants directed at free blacks was more than class antipathy. In Philadelphia the terrorization of the Negro population was called by white gangs "hunting the nigs."[86] Indeed the repeated use of the racial epithet "nigger" indicates that something more than dollars and cents was at stake in these struggles. Because America was a white man's country, access to its wealth was a white prerogative.[87] Black efforts to share in the bounty were viewed as acts of illegality and subversion. The Negro, being an alien or outsider, had no political or economic rights in American society. This is the real meaning of the African colonization movement: free Negroes had to be sent "back to Africa" because there was no place for them in a white man's country. This belief was held not only by native whites but also by immigrants. In fact, foreigners entering the United States before the Civil War, according to Reverend Ward, became "the bitterest of Negro-haters within fifteen days of their naturalization."[88] The Irish manifested a particularly virulent hatred of black people wherever they encountered them in the North in the antebellum decades. This antipathy carried over into the postwar period.[89]

Having come to America in search of a better life, the Irish initially were treated in a white supremacist country almost as though they were black: they became the white niggers of America. In the North the Irish were discriminated against socially, economically, and religiously. If they moved south, they were forced to do work normally reserved for slaves. "By mid-century," Dale T. Knobel has written, "language had built into American folk culture a sense that "Americans" and "Irish" were innately and permanently — physically — different from one another and that intelligence, morality, religious inclination, political affiliation, social conduct, and economic behavior were all derivatives of "race."[90] The derogatory language antebellum Americans used to describe the Irish "did not merely represent attitudes; they shaped attitudes."[91] By 1846 the author of a travel book could write that being an Irishman was "considered a crime in American belief."[92] The Irish, like black people, were victims of the "fiend prejudice."[93] Anglo-Americans between 1820 and 1860 came to think of the Irish as a "different race."[94] Other white immigrants such as the Germans were not derogated in this fashion.[95]

The treatment accorded the Irish in America represented a continuation of what they had known in the British Isles. In the eyes of the English, the Irish were a disgusting and totally unattractive people. Traveling in Ireland in 1860, Charles Kingsley called the Irish "human chimpanzees."[96] Although Kingsley made his observation in 1860, the practice of viewing the Irish as simians had begun as early as the reign of George III. By the time Queen Victoria ascended the British throne "the dominant stereotype" of the Irish, Perry Curtis, Jr., has written, "looked far more like an ape than man."[97] By caricaturing the Irish as apes, the English defined themselves as superior. The Irish, in short, served the same function in the British Isles that Negroes did in America. Nevertheless, although both the Irish and black people were treated as outsiders in pre–Civil War America, their common pariah status did not make them allies. In a society in which color was one badge of social preferment, the Irish were able to seek inclusion in ranks of the privileged white majority. An interracial alliance with black people would have stigmatized the children of Eire in the eyes of their white peers.[98] According to a class analysis, given their experience of oppression and discrimination, the Irish were prime candidates for some sort of alliance with blacks. At least this is what one would expect if people at all times acted rationally and were motivated solely by their class interest — if, as Michael Banton has put it, the idea of class "promised an ever-widening, patterning of group alliances based upon common relations to the ownership of the means of production."[99] History, however, did not follow this pattern in the nineteenth-century United States, where class consciousness remained a feeble force when compared with race. Reverend Ward captured the reality of this tension when he remarked:

> It turns out, that the man who on his native bog is unwashed and unshaved, a fellow lodger with his pig in a cabin too filthy for most people's stables or styes, is, when arriving in America, the Negro's birthplace, the free country for which the Negro fought and bled, one of the first to ridicule and abuse the Free Negro — the Negro, who has yet to learn how to sink into such depths of degradation as the Irishman has just escaped from. The bitterest, most heartless, most malignant, enemy of the Negro, is the Irish immigrant.[100]

If he were alive today Reverend Ward would probably be amused by the efforts of some historians to deny the centrality of race to the American experience by conflating it with class. This trend of thought has taken a curious and clever form in some recent studies in American and comparative history.[101] These studies take note of the fact that northern industrialists and slaveowners used a similar language to describe their respective work forces. But epithets such as "semi-civilized," "dirty," "vengeful," "violent," and "sensual" had different meanings when applied to black or white referents. To call this a language of class rather than taking note of precisely how a word is used ignores such questions of usage as context, inflection, and persistence of use. American capitalists could not make the distance between themselves and the white proletariat racial. Even when white men went on strike they had to be recognized, as *Harper's Weekly* acknowledged in 1877, as members of "the dominant race upon this continent."[102] The dominant race in North America before the Civil War was Caucasian, and five years of bloody struggle, plus twelve years of Reconstruction, did not alter this state of affairs.

The Civil War and Reconstruction constitute a hiatus in the evolution of American race relations, not a new departure. To be sure, black people were free, but as a former slave, George King, remarked, ". . . we are all free, but it don't mean we is white. And it don't mean we is equal."[103] The idea of Negro inferiority and subordination did not die easily in the postwar South. Five years of armed conflict had given the slaves "nothing but freedom" — and black freedom, as George King and more recently Eric Foner have told us, was marked by ambiguity.[104] In this sense the history of black southerners was characterized by more continuity than discontinuity, for slavery and the segregation that followed the demise of the "peculiar institution" were both based on the idea of Negro inferiority.[105] But while the hierarchy of the races remained essentially the same, the emancipation of the slaves introduced an element of indeterminacy into southern race relations. Before the war between the states, blacks and whites in the South lived in a world in which the free and unfree were distinguished by their color: in the antebellum South, whites had been free and blacks slaves.[106] Free Negroes were an anomaly because their freedom contradicted the basic premise of slave society that all blacks were slaves.[107] Like the emancipated Jewish populations of nineteenth-century France and Germany, Negroes assumed their new status as citizens under a cloud.[108]

Emancipation did not make either blacks or Jews citizens like their compatriots. In writing about nineteenth-century European Jewish history, Jacob Katz has captured this state of ambiguity most insightfully. "The relationship between the Jewish community," Katz writes, "and non-Jewish society was still strained by a heavy historical burden and social tension." Even though the Jews were free and "now a part of the general social framework," continues Katz, "having been recognized as citizens of the state — albeit an inferior class — the Jews were still a discernible and separate group and a problem to themselves and their environment."[109] Similarly the freed slaves were thought to be a problem to "themselves and their environment." Among southern whites, Sidney Andrews noted in 1866, there was an inability to "comprehend that freedom for the negro means the same thing as freedom for them."[110] Underlying this belief was the familiar idea that Negroes were physically and mentally different from whites. A delegate to the 1865 South Carolina constitutional convention expressed this idea forcefully when he remarked: "The negro is an animal; a higher sort of animal, to be sure, than the dog or the horse but, after all, an animal."[111] Political systems do not make beasts citizens, nor do they enfranchise them. For white southerners the Negro was a "troublesome animal; not a human being."[112] All emancipation did, in their view, was interrupt the Negroes' process of evolution. "With freedom, the negro en masse," Myrta Avary wrote, "relapsed promptly into the voodism of Africa."[113] The *Charleston Daily Courier*, October 1, 1866, decried the idea of emancipation and Negro equality. The paper told its readers:

> The African has been in, all ages, a savage or a slave. God created him inferior to the white man in form, color, and intellect, and no legislation or culture can make him his equal. You might as well expect to make the fox the equal of the lion in courage and strength, or the ass the equal of the horse in symmetry and fleetness. His color is black; his head covered with wool instead of hair, his form and features will not compare with the Caucasion race, and it is in vain to think of elevating him to the dignity of the white man. God has created a difference between the two races, and nothing can make him equal.[114]

Such white southerners thought of emancipation as a regressive act. It elevated what Roger Taney once called a "separate and degraded people," who were not ready for freedom and in some ways would never be, to a status they were unsuited for.[115] According to Alexander Stephens, freeing the slaves and attempting to make them the equal of whites was a "war against the decrees of nature."[116] But emancipation was more than this—it threatened to subject the South to something no other Caucasian population had suffered so far in the nineteenth century, that is, domination by people of color. Given white southern anxieties about color, sex, and white male authority, Reconstruction and what it portended represented a descent into chaos. To free the former slaves and endeavor to make blacks the legal equal of whites was folly, southerners thought. "As to negro suffrage, universal negro suffrage, the men that advocated such a measure as that must be lunatics or fools," a white man told John R. Dennett. "They had a poor idea of what made the glory and strength of true republican governments. The niggers were destitute of honesty; they didn't know the meaning of principles; they were ignorant and debased. . . ."[117] Voting was a white man's prerogative, and granting blacks the franchise demeaned the process of democratic government. Dennett, reporting from the South in 1865–66, heard a white farmer say, ". . . that a nigger was constituted pretty much like a mule, and was most serviceable and best contented when he had plenty of feed, plenty of work, and a little licking."[118]

In calling black people animals, nineteenth-century white southerners revealed a great deal about themselves and their society. One thing these comments tell us is that the standard Marxist litany about class does not work here. Both the ante- and postbellum South resemble places in Africa, Asia, Europe, and the Middle East where ethnic, racial, and religious differences took precedence over class divisions. Stated another way, race, ethnicity, and religion have been as much a force in history as class conflict. Even if one concedes, as I do, that there was class conflict in the South, one would have to mention the fact that this strife was sporadic and evanescent. It ebbed and flowed, whereas the issue of how to control black people seems to have been a constant in nineteenth-century white southern thought.

In giving race a primary place in southern history I am not embracing the view of U.B. Phillips, who claimed that race was the central theme of southern history.[119] What I want to suggest instead is that racial concerns were pervasive in both the pre- and postwar South,[120] and that white southerners' obsession with subordinating black people cut across class lines.[121] Class antipathies in the South were never sufficiently strong to challenge the practice of "white supremacy," which was far more than just a "slogan" for the southern blacks who were its victims.[122] Only a minority of the white populace was willing to give to black people the freedom and dignity they desired. Any Caucasian who treated black people as though they were social equals was ostracized and called a "nigger lover."[123] Why was this so?

The Negroes' outsider status, coupled with the trauma of emancipation, unleashed a host of fears in white southern society. A young man from Charlotte County, Virginia, for example, told Dennett that the franchise would enable black men to "vote themselves white wives."[124] Freeing the slaves, it would seem, was perceived by the former Confederates as more than a move toward social equality. On a deeper level the white South saw emancipation as a vehicle carrying them toward the horror of sexual equality.[125] According to a former senator and judge in Georgia, "no statutory law, no organic law, no military law supersedes the law of social necessity and social identity." For "social necessity," we can read "white supremacy"; for "social identity," the need to keep the races from mingling.[126] The pervasiveness of such fears of racial pollution make a class analysis problematic, indicating, as they do, a sensibility not amenable to rational suasion or class interest. The idea of Negro-ness in nineteenth-century America, both in the North and South, encompassed more than black people's relationship to the mode of production. Blacks, then, were not a class in the strict Marxist sense. Furthermore the Negroes' exclusion from political society works against any sort of class-like designation which presupposes a group's integration into the broader society. "This is a white man's government," an ex-colonel of a Virginia regiment told Whitelaw Reid, "and must be kept so till the end of time."[127] Andrew Johnson's presidency offered this possibility because he was "conservative on the nigger." "Johnson knows niggers," Reid heard in Atlanta. "He's not going to let any such cursed radicalism as inspired Lincoln trouble him. If Johnson had been President, we wouldn't have been embarrassed by any infernal Emancipation Proclamation."[128]

Commenting on the state of American race relations a Maryland paper, the *Cecil Whig*, observed in 1869: "There is nothing the American people seem to fear so much as a nigger. . . ."[129] In the postwar South this fear was expressed not only in legislation such as the black codes but also in what Bertram Doyle called the "etiquette" of race relations. "The law stipulated that the negro was to be a citizen," Doyle says, "but custom . . . defined both the forms of behavior expected of Negroes and their place in the social system."[130] As slaves, black people had not been allowed to sit down in the presence of their master and mistress. In addressing whites, slaves were required to call them "Massa" or "Misses."[131] Regardless of their age bondsmen and bondswomen were either "boy" or "girl"; they never grew up.[132] When a black person became old and was given the soubriquet "uncle" or "auntie," these titles did not denote affection, only powerlessness. White southern expectation after the war was that these patterns of deference would continue. The Negro as a free person was still expected to be obedient, and any deviation from the proscribed pattern of deference was deemed to be insolence.[133] Efforts at self-improvement by freed slaves were construed as "trying to act like white people" or "putting on airs."[134] One former rebel told Sidney Andrews: "The nigger is crazy to ride, — to own an old mule and old cart, and to be seen driving through the streets, . . . it seems to give grave offense to the gentry of the state that the negro likes riding better than walking, that he will insist on buying a poor old mule and a poor old cart and going into business for himself."[135] The freed slaves abandonment of "nigger ways" infuriated their former masters. "I wish they'd shoot 'em all," Dennett heard a white woman say. "I am glad when I hear o' one of 'em got out o' the way," the lady continued. "If I could get up tomorrow morning and hear that every nigger in the county was dead, I'd just jump up and down."[136]

Such an intense sense of negrophobia points to a racialism that was virtually uncontrollable. To paraphrase Joel Williamson, race in the nineteenth-century South was a problem of the "mind" and "body."[137] As free people blacks drove white men and women crazy; lynching was the most extreme public expression of this insanity. Embodying simultaneously the aspects of a carnival and an auto-da-fé, lynchings eradicated the out-of-place "niggers" that caused white southerners such unease.[138] "In my county white folks is white folks, and niggers is brought up to know their place," exclaimed a white woman to Dennett.[139] But even when black people stayed in their place, southern whites did not respect them. Whitelaw Reid expressed a hope shared by few former Confederates when he remarked that once the freedmen were "settled" and acquired "some of the rewards of steady industry" they would become like "any other class of laborers."[140] To the ex-rebels this was utter nonsense. White direction, not black initiative, had made black people efficient and productive laborers. "A nigger hated work, and had no ambition; he would do just enough to keep him from actual starvation," a North Carolinian explained to John R. Dennett.[141] Commenting on the freed blacks' future prospects in 1866, Dennett wrote:

It has not always been found the fact in other countries that a laboring class, because its labor is honestly bought and paid for, necessarily obtains all its social and political rights. And no such class in other countries, at least in modern days, has been opposed by prejudices so strong as those against which the Negro will have to contend. Indeed, in my opinion, what he has gained already cannot yet be regarded as his permanent and secure possession.[142]

What Dennett captured in this observation was the peculiarity of the black's status in America and the South in the postwar period.

The recent works of Professors Fields, Hahn, Robinson, and Wiener miss this point.[143] Concerned with demonstrating that America and the South were not exceptions to a world-wide pattern of class conflict, their studies have tended to deemphasize race and submerge the importance of class and racial oppression in a larger construct of class antipathies. Jonathan Wiener does this, for example, in his essay "Class Structure and Economic Development in the American South, 1865–1955."[144] "From the perspective of class analysis," Wiener writes, "blacks suffered the greatest exploitation and oppression, but the system of labor restrictions centering on debt peonage — requiring an individual to labor against his will to satisfy a debt — expanded to include whites as well. The system was, therefore, not exclusively racial in orientation — all whites dominating all blacks — but a class system — white planters dominating tenants of both races, with blacks forming the most oppressed part of the working class."[145] This is very interesting, but it ignores the larger context in which Negro oppression occurred after the Civil War. The fact that poor whites and blacks occupied the same economic niche does not mean, as Wiener argues, that they were treated the same. In fact, the rulers of the New South treated their landless white tenants differently from their black employees. As Charles Flynn has written: ". . . the South's elaborate system of racial etiquette and prejudice preserved an important degree of respectability for landless whites and placed them apart and above their black counterparts." Flynn comes to the heart of this differentiation when he says: "For a white tenant to be called 'mister' while a black, if he were aged and white-haired, at best received the honorific title 'uncle' reflected different social status and a different latitude in behavior that had real substance. Landless whites received a social and economic dividend from discrimination that reinforced their long standing commitment" to white supremacy.[146]

Southern white adherence to the principle of white supremacy transcended class position. It is beside the point to describe it, as Barbara Fields has, as a "slogan that cannot have meant the same to all white people," or to ascribe varying types and degrees of racism to different categories of southerners.[147] In attempting to characterize racism as somehow shaped or determined by the "social position of its proponents" Fields and others are obscuring the vital point that whatever variant forms it took, white racism was an utterly pervasive element of southern society before and after the Civil War, one which effectively blocked the way toward social, economic, and legal equality for blacks.[148] Writing from the South in 1865–66, John R. Dennett noted a unanimity of opinion among white southerners about the former slaves. "So far as

I have seen," wrote Dennett, "all native Southerners, the poorest and most degraded equally with the rich, and the people of the most undoubted unionism as well as secessionist, unaffectedly and heartily despise the Negroes."[149] Sidney Andrews noted a similar distaste for black people when he observed of white southerners that ". . . not one man in five thousand proposed to give them all the rights of men and women, and scarcely one in twenty thousand would invest them with the rights of citizenship."[150] J.T. Trowbridge, traveling in East Tennessee, reported that whites in that section of the state ". . . though opposed to slavery and secession do not like niggers. There is at this day more prejudice against color among the middle and poorer classes — the "union" men, who owned few or no slaves — than among the planters who owned them by the scores and hundreds. . . ."[151] Finally, a southern judge calling himself "conservative" testified to a congressional committee in 1871 that, on his circuit, "In some sections of the State there is a feeling of personal hostility to the negro; and in some portions of my circuit they will not let a negro live; that is, it is a white population; and they do not want to come in contact with the negro . . . they want to have an exclusively white society."[152] In attempting to prettify the reality of this pervasive postwar racism in the South, a younger generation of southern historians does both itself and its field of study a disservice. For what these scholars have done is deny the importance of what white southerners were most proud of, that is, the color of their skin. Possession of a white skin gave one status regardless of wealth or social position. To ignore this in the study of nineteenth-century southern history is dangerously misleading. The late Anthony West has called the practitioners of this act of imagination "fabalists," who "deal with unacceptable truths, by modifying them again and again until they have been transformed into more negotiable material."[153] But this act of revision has a more sinister result, for it represents a rewriting of American history so drastic as to trivialize the struggle of black people for freedom and equality. The efforts of nineteenth-century American blacks to enjoy the rights granted them in the Thirteenth, Fourteenth, and Fifteenth amendments proceeded from a different context than the efforts of poor whites and yeomen to achieve economic justice. The two struggles, although parallel, had different etiologies, and a class analysis blurs this aspect of American history. Morgan J. Kousser recognized this when he wrote ". . . the tactic of identifying Negro and white agriculturalists as co-victims of the same economic system ignores the fact that Negroes were often more concerned with social and political than with economic discrimination."[154]

If black people, as Kousser indicates, were more occupied with "social and political" concerns, where does the current emphasis on class in southern history come from? It derives from an exaggeration of the attention paid to class conflict in the magisterial work of C. Vann Woodward.[155] In a series of books which redefined the shape and content of southern historiography, Woodward pointed out that the South's history could not be encompassed by U.B. Phillips's idea of racism as the central theme, and that it had been marked more by discontinuity than continuity.[156] In unraveling the tangled skein of postbellum southern history, Woodward paid close attention to class and racial conflict. "It was an entirely safe assumption that for a long time to come race consciousness would divide," Woodward wrote in 1951, "more than class consciousness would unite, Southern labor. Fifty strikes against the employment of Negro labor in the period from 1882 to 1900 testify to white labor's determination to draw a color line of its own."[157] In his biography of Tom Watson, written thirteen years before, however, Woodward argued that class posed a serious challenge to racial division in the South, and that Tom Watson and the Populists offered voters an alternative to the racist demagoguery of southern Democrats.[158] Within the Populist movement, Woodward wrote, poor blacks and whites marched shoulder to shoulder, in a rare exercise of interracial cooperation. (On one occasion, for example, Watson's black supporter H.S. Doyle took refuge on the *Agrarian Rebel's* estate, and to insure Doyle's saftey Watson dispatched "riders on horseback for assistance."[159]) The work of Charles Crowe, Robert Saunders, and Barton Shaw suggest that Woodward's positive depiction of Populism needs to be moderated, however.[160] The Populists were alienated Democrats and negrophobes, who wanted to use the Negro vote as the Democrats and Republicans had, to maintain themselves in power. They represented no break with the racial attitudes of the southern past and offered no alternative to black people. Robert Saunders has written of the party in Virginia that:

> Based on the organization efforts in Virginia and elsewhere in the South, it appears safe to conclude that the Negro never came close to being an equal partner with his white Populist colleague. The Negro never performed more than a smattering of duties, held anywhere near the percentage of offices his numbers warranted, nor had any real voice in shaping programs and decisions in the Populist party. Undoubtedly too much has been made of the political cooperation between white Populists and Negroes, especially if one means cooperation in the machinery of a mutual party on the basis of equality.[161]

Barton Shaw has shown that in Georgia some Populists were hostile to the former slaves, even donning the regalia of the Klan and terrorizing the freedmen.[162] Populist hostility to blacks can be explained in terms of the party members' fear that their organization would be labeled the "nigger party." No political institution bearing this epithet could expect to attract white support.[163] For most southerners equal access to the polling booth was the beginning of social equality between blacks and whites with the attendant threat of miscegenation.[164] I have already indicated the extent of southern whites' obsessive speculation about the subject of the Negroes' sexual desires, which produced such fantasies as the assertion of one white southern male that Negro men raped white women because of a "want of virtue among their own females."[165] In a society in which this kind of self-serving delusion operated as reality, how was a politics based on a rational calculation of self-interest possible?

If racial and psycho-sexual fears made a politics based on class interest impossible for whites, similar anxieties also existed in the black community. Black people feared not only the Populist leaders but also their followers. In Georgia, for example, W.A. Pledger, a black Republican, opposed cooperation between his people and the Populists in these terms: "The men who have lynched the colored people in the past; the men who have shot and robbed the colored people; the men who precipitated the 'Camilla riot' years ago and who marshalled the red shirter and night riders are now the followers and shouters of Peek and his crowd."[166] The poor whites who were drawn to the Populist banner were the ex-slaves' worst foes. "Poor whites," a Freedman's Bureau official testified in 1866, were the Negroes' ". . . enemies. It is from these he suffers most. In a state of slavery they hated him; and now that he is free, there is no abatement of the sentiment."[167] Another witness to conditions in the South stated that ". . . it was a common saying amongst the Negroes before the war that they would rather be a nigger than a poor white man."[168] Given the suspicions and fears that characterized race relations during slavery and after, there was no common ground on which southern whites and blacks could meet in the 1890s. So deeply ingrained was the freedmen's fear of whites that one black man told a Senate committee: "We do not want any social equality here." He went on to say that black people did not want "to go into white people's houses and mingle with them as social equals."[169] Another witness before this same investigatory group voiced opposition to social equality for different reasons.

> Here is the only thing that we are troubled about now, about civil rights. A colored man and his wife may go to work to get a little home, may go hungry and naked to educate a daughter, the dearest treasure that they have got, and the very moment that she begins to come up there is an inroad made upon her by the whites of this country, and we have got no redress in the world. They can't deny that. Now, I want as much civil rights and rules to regulate and protect my family as any white man does, and if I catch a man under such circumstances I won't hurt him but once!
>
> The CHAIRMAN. You have that right beyond question, and should exercise it.
>
> The WITNESS. That is what we want, to protect the virtue of our girls. That is the rights I want. I don't want no social equality with

the white people, and I don't want them to have none with me. I see
the influence of this thing everyday. There has been a time when
they were opposed to such things, but now that we are free the
parents of the children can't even protect their children, and there
ain't a white man here can deny it. That is the trouble in this country. Give the nigger a chance and he is going to till the white man's
soil, and he is going to keep out of his house, too. There is some
fools, of course, but generally if they let the nigger alone he won't
interfere with them.[170]

Obviously what these Negroes wanted was the equal protection of
the law. They did not want to be closely associated with whites. But
there were other black people who looked forward to an association
with their white peers. Indeed, some blacks thought that their hard
work would lead to harmonious race relations and that there would
be racial bonding along class lines. The chief proponent of this
point of view in postbellum black America was Booker T. Washington.[171] Washington's program of social uplift was similar to the
efforts of nineteenth-century French and German Jews to assimilate. That is, it was predicated upon the assumption that when black
people abandoned those cultural traits that distinguished them
from whites they would be accepted by their oppressors. Time
would reveal the insubstantial base underlying this strategy.

Washington's program of social rehabilitation was an exercise
in blaming the victim. He told black people that their problems
were of their own making. Placed in a broader context, Washington's criticism of black people resembles the indictment of French
Jews articulated by Bernard Lazare in the 1890s. Lazare told his
people that "the general causes of anti-Semitism have always resided in Israel itself." Jews throughout history had been "unsoci-
able" and "exclusive," according to Lazare. Refusing to assimilate,
they had "isolated themselves from the rest of mankind."[172] Washington castigated blacks in similar terms for being unclean, un-
punctual, and for failing in general to internalize the values of
white bourgeois restraint and uplift. The answer to the Negro's
problem, Washington thought, lay in individual merit. He wrote
". . . I am conscious of the fact that mere connection with what

is known as a superior race will not permanently carry an individual forward unless he has individual worth, and mere connection with what is regarded as an inferior race will not finally hold an individual back if he possesses intrinsic individual merit . . . that merit, no matter under what skin found, is, in the long run, recognized and rewarded."[173] If the Negro worked hard he would be accepted into the mainstream of American life.

This program, as I have written elsewhere, "was based on a confusion between culture and politics."[174] The Negro's problem in the South vis-à-vis whites was not culture, it was color, and what blackness had historically connoted and denoted in southern society. Washington erred when he thought that class interest would override racism, that the rulers of the New South would give educated and propertied blacks the vote and disenfranchise poor whites so that the vote would be the exclusive privilege of middle- and upper-class blacks and whites. "More and more I am convinced that the final solution of our race problem will be for each state," Washington wrote, "that finds it necessary to change the law bearing upon the franchise to make the law apply with absolute honesty, and without opportunity for double dealing or evasion, to both races alike."[175] This was unfounded optimism. The South's commitment to white supremacy was total, and no exceptions to this principle were to be made. "Educated or ignorant, rich or poor, the niggers must be kept down," Whitelaw Reid was told after the war.[176] The South did not deviate from this rule between 1865 and 1900. When viewed from this perspective, Populism was not an aberration or deviation from the idea of white on top, black on the bottom. It was a continuation of the old mechanisms of racial control in a new guise.

The recent emphasis on class analysis in southern history fails to note the major weakness of Washington's program of racial uplift: its inability to protect even the most successful and zealous adherents of Washington's ideology. Between 1889 and 1946 almost four thousand black people were lynched.[177] A large number of these acts of terror occurred in the South and were directed at successful blacks. People who were climbing the American ladder of success were targeted for mob action. Ebenezer Fowler, the wealthiest black man in Issaquena County, Mississippi, was shot and killed on January 30, 1885, by an armed body of white men. Fowler's crime was writing to a white woman, an indiscretion which he paid for with his life.[178] In 1892 three black men were lynched in Memphis, Tennessee, after opening a grocery that competed with a white business. Ida Wells-Barnett has written of these men: "They were peaceful, law-abiding citizens and energetic businessmen. . . . They believed the problem was to be solved by eschewing politics and putting money in the purse."[179] For their efforts these blacks "were secretly taken from jail and lynched." "The Negroes were getting too independent," whites said; "we must teach them a lesson."[180] In 1898, the appointment of a black postmaster in Lake City, South Carolina, precipitated a race riot. The postmaster's house was set afire and three of his children were shot as they fled their burning home.[181] These were not isolated incidents; they carried over into the twentieth century. In 1904, for example, several of Booker T. Washington's followers in Mississippi found that their success infuriated white mobs. Isaiah T. Montgomery, a resident of Mound Bayou, Mississippi, wrote to Washington on September 6, 1904, about a recent assault on the property and life of Reverend C.A. Buchanan. Montgomery reported:

> Reverend Buchanan has the best appointed printing establishment of any colored man in the State, and conducts a Baptist newspaper . . . and was no doubt prospering, his daughter was his cashier and Book-Keeper, they kept a Horse and Buggy, which the young woman used frequently in going to and from work; they kept a decent house and a piano; a mass meeting of whites decided that the mode of living practiced by the Buchanan family had a bad effect on the cooks and washerwomen, who aspired to do likewise, and became less disposed to work for whites.[182]

Why were prosperous blacks singled out for such attacks? The answer cannot be that class antagonism in America is often expressed in racial violence. Such a nonsensical conclusion would avoid the fact that Negroes have been the victims of white violence regardless of their class position in the nineteenth and twentieth centuries. The assaults did not emanate solely from middle-class whites who terrorized their black peers. The racial terror black people suffered was directed at the entire Negro community. Middle-class blacks were the vanguard of something whites feared in general: "niggers" out of their place. In this sense the history of emancipated Negroes parallels the treatment accorded upwardly mobile European Jews after 1798. "Once they were conceived of as strangers," Jacob Katz has written of this anomaly, "no economic or other achievement was to their credit: rather they counted as trespassers on the sphere of life of the autocthonous population."[183] Free black people were "matter out of place." Their emancipation was an affront to southern white freedom. Booker T. Washington did not understand that his program was perceived as subversive of a natural order in which black people were to remain forever subordinate or unfree. Steven Hahn is mistaken when he writes that "racial attitudes of upcountry yeomen constituted an historically specific variant of broader class attitudes: those of small property holders toward the propertyless poor. . ." The antipathy of the yeomen, as this essay has argued, was much broader than Hahn suggests. Even when blacks were not "laborers devoid of means" they "terrified smallholders."[184] Race, not class, was the source of this unease.

What I have done in this chapter is argue that for the nineteenth century race is a legitimate category of explanation for human action. Sutton Griggs understood this when, in commenting on the possibility of interracial political alliance in the South, he wrote that whites were ". . . determined to keep undimmed their white complexion, the physical badge of membership in the white race. And the problem of keeping Negro blood out of the veins of the white race is the paramount problem with the southern white man, and to it all other questions, whether economic, political or social are made to yield."[185] A history of the United States and the South that ignores or denies the importance of race in shaping American thought and action is a fable. Histories based on class analysis do this because they are based on an exclusionary paradigm of history. By identifying class conflict as real and structural and concomitantly arguing that race is fictitious, mystifying, and superstructural, this method of analysis has created a world that never existed. Critics of this argument will say that I have ignored the theoretical constructs of race and class. Some of the work I have criticized in these pages claims to be demonstrating the interaction of race and class. In fact what this scholarship has done is to create an analytical monster with a "somewhat oversized head" (class) and "wizened body and limbs" (race). Just how these parts interact is unclear. What is evident, however, is that class seems to overwhelm everything else in the construct. "History should be informed by theory, not consumed by it."[186]

Finally, how many niggers did Karl Marx know? Possibly just one. Karl Marx's son-in-law, Paul Lafargue, was a black man born in Cuba, in 1842. Lafargue was the husband of Marx's second daughter.[187]

The Virtuoso Illusionist: Marcus Garvey

In her splendid novel *A Short Walk,* Alice Childress has the following exchange between two characters, Estelle and Cora:

> "Who is Marcus Garvey?"
> "A little black fella from down Jamaica.
> Bought hisself a one-way ticket to New York and got off the boat
>   promisin to take Negroes back to Africa."
> "For what?"
> "To be royalty — kings, queens, lords and ladies — and to own all
>   of Africa. Cecil is one a his right hand men. One damn fool
>   in the service of another."[1]

This fictional passage is insightful because it suggests that some
ordinary working-class black Americans were skeptical of both
Garvey and his program of racial redemption. This is a point
often ignored by students of the Garvey movement, who in their
efforts to create a usable past for American blacks have given
Garvey a central place in the pantheon of American black nationalist heroes.[2] Garvey has been called a "Black Moses" and
described as a revitalizer of American black politics; it has been
said of him that he "stirred the imagination of the Negro masses
as no Negro ever had."[3] Garvey, as one of his followers remarked,
gave "my people backbone where they had wishbone."[4] What all
of these characterizations have in common is an assumption that
Garvey transformed American black consciousness between his

arrival in 1916 and his deportation in 1927, when he was con-
victed of mail fraud in connection with the Black Star Steamship
Company.

What I propose to argue in this chapter is that the Garvey
movement was racist and reactionary, and not an expression of
American black nationalism. Despite the fact that some American blacks were attracted to Garvey's UNIA, it was a West Indian
movement, more Afro-British than Afro-American in both its
symbolism and its ideology. As Harold Cruse has written, Garveyism "was not an Afro-American nationalist movement engaged
in an historical confrontation with the realities of the American
situation out of which it sprung. Garveyism was Afro-British nationalism functioning outside its historical British empire context, hence avoiding British confrontation."[5] The forces that produced Garvey were world-wide phenomena and not specific to
America. Garveyism as a social movement was part of the historical process that in Europe produced the new dictatorships of
the 1920s and 1930s. In short, Garveyism promised to reorder the
world for its adherents, including those black Americans who
joined the UNIA because they felt betrayed by their country and
traditional leaders.

Who then was Marcus Malchus Garvey?[6] He was born in the
town of St. Ann's Bay, in northern Jamaica, on August 17, 1887.[7]
Garvey's parents were members of the Jamaican lower middle class.
His father was a mason and his mother a seamstress. At the time of
Garvey's birth, his parents — Sarah Richards and Malchus Mosiah
Garvey — were not married. Their certificate of marriage, dated
December 15, 1889, indicates that they were not married until two
years after his birth. Illegitimacy may have had a profound effect
on Garvey, who later — in good bourgeois fashion — condemned
pre-marital sex among Negroes and mulattoes.

Any study of Garvey, his career, and the organization he founded
to redeem the race must begin with the fact that he was the child
of what he called, in an article published in 1923, "black Negroes."[8]
Garvey was proud of the fact that his family tree was free from
the taint of miscegenation. In his native Jamaica, society was

stratified according to color, which served as an indicator of social standing and mobility. Within this system whites occupied
the top position; "coloreds," or browns, were next in order of
precedence; and blacks were at the bottom of the hierarchy. This
tripartite system was different from the racial order in the United
States, where people with any Negro ancestry were all grouped
together both socially and legally by the white majority. Unlike
the West Indies and Latin America, where any non-black ancestry automatically removed a person from the black community, the United States did not develop a mulatto escape hatch.[9]

Growing up in Jamaica, Garvey claimed that until the age of
fourteen he was unaware of differences "between black and white"
and was also oblivious to "race feeling and [problems]."[10] He
learned that there was a race problem when the parents of a white
playmate decided "to separate us and draw the color line." The
little girl was sent to Europe to be educated; her parents told her,
Garvey writes, "that she was never to write or try to get in touch
with me, for I was a nigger." It was at this time, Garvey says, "that
I found out for the first time that there was some difference in
humanity, and that there were different races, each having its own
separate and distinct social life." Subsequent experience and study
were to reinforce Garvey's awareness and understanding of the
racial differences among humankind.[11]

When Garvey was fourteen his family's financial problems forced
him to drop out of school. During the next few years, as a printer's
apprentice in Kingston, he acquired the skills that would later make
him an accomplished editor, propagandist, and public speaker.
It was probably during this period, although the connections are
not clear, that Garvey became acquainted with the ideas of "racial autonomy" and "African redemption," concepts that were later
to be important components of his program of racial uplift.[12] By
the time he was twenty, Garvey was a master printer and foreman
at one of the largest Jamaican printing establishments, the P.A.
Benjamin Co. In 1907, when the Printers' Union in Kingston struck
for higher wages, Garvey quickly became a leader of the strike
and worked to arouse public sympathy for the strikers. After the

strike was broken, Garvey—the only foreman who had supported
the walkout—found himself blacklisted. This experience with
unions may have soured Garvey on unionization, because later
on, as a race leader, he would be hostile to unions.[13]

Sometime during the winter of 1910-11, Garvey emigrated to
Central America. During a brief sojourn in the Canal Zone, Garvey tried to radicalize the sixty thousand Jamaicans living there.
He also founded two newspapers during his year-long stay in Central America: *La Nacionale* [*sic*] in Costa Rica and *La Prensa*
in Panama. In the pages of these papers, Garvey publicized the
wretched living and working conditions of Jamaicans who had
emigrated to the area. During this experience, as Boyd C. James
has written, Garvey "came face-to-face with what he believed to
be the foundation for the success of Western European nations—
race unity. And in the enclaves of the Canal Zone where his people
were not united, he saw them suffer and perish."[14] Upon leaving
Central America, Garvey returned briefly to Jamaica before traveling to London.[15] He says of this trip, "I set sail for Europe to find
out if it was different there, and again I found the same stumbling-
block—'you're black.'"[16] In London, Garvey met a number of
African intellectuals, students, and seamen who told him about
the plight of black people in their homelands, corroborating his
experiences in Jamaica and Central America. All the evidence
confirmed that black people were the ones farthest down.[17]

During his stay in London, Garvey read Booker T. Washington's *Up From Slavery*. According to Garvey the book had a profound effect upon him "and then my doom—if I may call it—of
being a race leader dawned upon me in London. . . . I asked,
'Where is the black man's government?' 'Where is his king and
his kingdom?' 'Where is his President, his country, and his am-
bassador, his army, his navy, his men of big affairs?' I could not
find them, and then I declared, 'I will help to make them.'"[18]
Despite this grandiloquent statement, Garvey's decision to become a race leader should not be attributed solely to his reading of
Booker T. Washington's book. The powerful testimony of the other
blacks he met while in London also played an important role.[19]

By 1914, Garvey was ready to elevate the race. He left England and returned to Jamaica on July 15, 1914. Five days after he returned home, Garvey founded the Universal Negro Improvement and Conservation Association and the African Communities League.[20] He adumbrated his organization's uplift functions in a speech delivered to the Association's first annual meeting in 1915.

> The bulk of our people are in darkness and are really unfit for good society. To the cultured mind the bulk of our people are contemptible — that is to say, they are entirely outside the pale of cultured appreciation. You know this to be true, so we need not get uneasy through prejudice. Go into the country parts of Jamaica and you see there villainy and vice of the worst kind, immorality, obeah and all kinds of dirty things are part of the avocation of a large percentage of our people, and we, the few of cultured tastes can in no way save the race from infamy in a balanced comparison with other people, for the standard of races or of anything else is not arrived at by the few who are always the exceptions, but by the majority.
>
> Well, this society has set itself the task to go among the people and help them up to a better state of appreciation among the cultured classes, and raise them to the standard of civilized approval.[21]

As this speech indicates, Garvey did not base his awakening of black people, whether in Jamaica or the United States, on a celebration or appreciation of African folk culture. He saw these forms, Robert Hill has written, "as inimical to racial progress and as evidence of the retardation that for generations has made for racial weakness."[22] Garvey revealed his contempt for African-American cultural forms when he remarked: "Spiritual and Jazz Music are credited to the Negro . . . simply because we did not know better music."[23] What Garvey wanted to do was raise black people to what he called the "standard of civilized approval," a euphemism for a replication of the cultural forms of the British Empire.[24] This rejection of black culture, so striking for a supposedly "nationalist" movement, is one of the chief characteristics of Garveyism.

Although Garvey claimed in his 1915 speech "that it [was] not [his] intention nor the intention of the Society to belabor any race question," race soon came to be the heart of his movement in Jamaica.[25] In attempting to improve the conditions of the Jamaican black masses, Garvey angered members of the colored Jamaican middle class, who felt threatened by his efforts to organize Jamaican Negroes on the basis of their race. The coloreds did not want to be grouped with the darker Jamaican underclass. Thus, the struggle between the colored and black Jamaicans was based on both class differences and racial differences.[26] Ultimately, the rejection of Garvey's program by the Jamaican coloreds forced the aspiring race leader to come to America.

Garvey arrived in the United States on March 23, 1916. He came to America to speak with Booker T. Washington, but the Wizard of Tuskegee had died in the fall of 1915.[27] Garvey's arrival in the United States coincided with the transformation of what historically had been a southern problem into a national one. Since the end of slavery in 1865, there had been a slow and steady migration of black people out of the southeastern part of the United States. But with the coming of World War I, the emigration of blacks from the South was to exceed earlier Negro exoduses from the land of bondage. Between 1916 and 1918 an estimated half-million blacks moved to the North in search of a better life.[28] The movement of black people out of the South occurred at a time of great demand for unskilled labor in northern industries. Black people filled this gap until 1919, when there was a tapering off in the demand. The arrival of large numbers of black migrants in northern urban centers placed great strain on these cities' housing facilities. Those black people who came north in search of better economic opportunities and civil liberties soon had their hopes dashed. Although the United States was fighting to make the world safe for democracy, black people soon found their quest for freedom in the new Canaan land to be fruitless.

In 1917, the quiet of the city of East St. Louis, Illinois, was torn by a bloody race riot led by whites who resented the fact that blacks were employed in factories holding government war contracts.[29] Rioting was not the only form of racial violence during the war years. Lynching also became more prevalent. There were thirty-eight Negro victims of mob violence nationally in 1917, and, in 1918, nineteen blacks were lynched.[30] These acts of terror presaged what James Weldon Johnson called the "red summer" of 1919. From June until December of 1919 there were twenty-five race riots in the United States.[31] These outbursts occurred in all parts of the country, in large and small urban centers. What this violence represented was an attempt on the part of certain sectors of the white populace to reestablish control over black people, control that the whites thought they had lost as a result of World War I and the urbanization of blacks. A white man speaking to a crowd of Negroes in New Orleans in 1918 made this point with devastating brutality: "You niggers are wondering how you are going to be treated after the war. Well, I'll tell you, you are going to be treated exactly like you were before the war; this is a white man's country and we expect to rule."[32]

Some American historians have concluded that the growing racial tension at the end of the second decade of the twentieth century provided Garvey with a very large and receptive audience of disillusioned American blacks. "By 1919," Edmund D. Cronon has written, "American Negroes were ready for any program that would tend to restore even a measure of their lost dignity and self-respect."[33] But while this was undoubtedly true for some American blacks, it is questionable to assume that Garveyism attracted the huge following that has often been attributed to it.

First of all, no satisfactory estimate of the size of Garvey's following has yet been made.[34] Measuring the strength of the movement is particularly difficult because, in a culture as pervasively racist as this one was, any meeting or gathering of black people was bound to be exaggerated because it was thought unusual. In other words, the very uniqueness of the UNIA may have contributed to the public perception of it as "the largest [and] broadest mass movement in Afro-American history."[35] Furthermore, the presence of a large West Indian population in the United States, and the accompanying hostility of American blacks toward

West Indians, make it unlikely that a West Indian leader could have attracted a large American following.

Historians and others who have seen Garvey as the leader of an aroused American Negro populace have conveniently ignored the fact that the 1920s was a period of intense xenophobia on the part of American blacks. Those Negroes, for example, who migrated from the South to the North were not received by northern blacks with open arms. The migrants increased the competition for jobs and housing, and northern Negroes resented this competition.[36] The arrival of West Indian immigrants exacerbated this problem. Concomitant with and pre-dating black migration from the South was a movement of West Indian Negroes from the Caribbean into northeastern urban centers. During the first three decades of the twentieth century the number of black aliens and non-native black residents in the United States increased from 54,737 to 181,981.[37] Black Americans from different parts of the country may not have liked each other, but there was one thing they could agree upon: job opportunities in the northern cities should go to American citizens first. To these people the West Indians were foreigners and aliens, not brothers.[38]

American blacks found the islanders pushy, aggressive, clannish, insensitive, and self-seeking. Underlying their hostility was the fact that the Americans were less well educated than many of the West Indians, a number of whom were skilled artisans, business people, and professionals. Because of American racism, many of the immigrants were unable to pursue their original vocations and therefore put their talents to work in businesses within the black community. Their success earned them both the envy and enmity of American blacks. American Negroes living in New York often referred to the West Indians as "the black Jews of Harlem."[39] The black immigrants were stereotyped as energetic, frugal, thrifty, and tenacious.[40] Since the nineteenth century, black Americans had attributed these same qualities to Jews; an attribution expressive of both admiration and distaste.[41] The fact that West Indians were perceived in similar terms suggests that American blacks on some level ultimately came to think of the islanders as untrustworthy — as a people whose dedication to business meant they had to be dealt with cautiously because they might take advantage of one.

Business was not the only issue that divided the emigrants from American blacks. Coming from a more cosmopolitan racial environment, the West Indians were extremely vocal in their criticisms of North American racial mores and American blacks' acceptance of these customs. They ridiculed American blacks and pointed out that as citizens of another country, West Indians could always get the British Consular Service to protest against any insult or injustice they received from white Americans. In the eyes of American blacks, the emigrants were opportunists who had come to the United States simply to make money. The West Indians themselves lent credence to this belief by boasting that they did not have to stay in America and also by refusing to become naturalized citizens.[42] This tendency to remain aloof from black American society, and — in some cases, at least — to criticize a racial situation they imperfectly understood increased the antagonism between the two black communities.

In response to this antagonism, American blacks resorted to the black American tradition of ridicule. Harlemites said that when a West Indian "got ten cents above a beggar he opened a business."[43] Epithets such as "ring tail" and "King Mon," "monkey chaser" and "cockney" were aimed at the emigrants. "When a monkey-chaser dies / Don't need no undertaker / Just throw him in de Harlem River / He'll float back to Jamaica."[44] A popular song of the mid-twenties, "West Indian Blues," indicates the depth of American black antipathy toward West Indians:

Done give up de bestes' job
A running' elevator,
I told my boss "mon" I'd be back
Sometime soon or later.
When I git back to dis great land,
You better watch me Harvey,
'Cause 'm gonna be a great big "mon"
Like my frien Marcus Garvey.[45]

In many ways, Garvey exemplified the stereotyped image that American blacks held of West Indians. Both intolerant and ignorant of the American racial problem, Garvey merely transferred to the United States the difficulties he had encountered in Jamaica. He did this because for him the race question was framed in terms of an "unproblematically unified black identity, unfissured by differences and immune to determinants of . . . country. . . ."[46] According to Garvey there was "absolutely no difference between the native African and the American and West Indian Negroes, in that [they are] descendants from one common family stock."[47]

Such statements demonstrate that Garvey's vision of history was at once both static and evolutionary. It was static in the sense that he saw black people as somehow undifferentiated by time. Evolution's role in this process was that in the "progression" of the race, Africans and their descendants who had contact with European and North American civilization had progressed more quickly, successfully, and correctly than Africans who had had no such contact.[48] Africans were, in short, a "great mass of unprepared people" about to destroy themselves.[49] Therefore, it was the duty of the race's vanguard to return home and save their brothers.

Garvey's success in articulating his idea of African redemption lay in a skillful manipulation of myth as history. Ancient societies, Eugen Weber has written, "shared a common language of symbol and myth. In modern societies these are lacking or not generally recognized; they have to be rediscovered, reinvented, reasserted."[50] History plays an important role in this process, for "it has become the theology of our time, a reservoir in which one delves to find the particular traditions that might suit one's ends — for even myths must have some root in reality."[51] Garvey's modern myth differed from that of the ancients "in that it [was] not the expression of a truth, otherwise too profound for mass comprehension, but a manipulative device. The myth or symbol of an earlier day had been a parable, describing some reality considered too profound, too complex, too abstruse."[52] Garvey's myth, like modern myth, ran counter to reality, which it ignored and distorted to change the status quo. Garvey, like George Sorel, wanted to create "an entirely epic state of mind and at the same time bend all the energies of the mind" to his will.[53] Garvey's end or goal was purely pragmatic—the creation of a new world order.

Spouting slogans like "Up You Mighty Race," "Africa for the Africans," "Wake Up Ethiopia," and "Wake Up Africa," Garvey arrived in New York in 1916. These slogans and Garvey's program of African redemption are generally believed to have made him the leader of the largest mass movement of blacks in American history. Given the antipathies I discussed earlier, however, this generalization needs to be qualified. Nor can the Garvey movement be placed squarely in the tradition of American black emigrationism or colonization.[54] Garveyism drew on this tradition, but in some ways its program was profoundly different from the work of Alexander Crummell, Paul Cuffe, Martin Delany, and Henry M. Turner. All of these men had been interested in redeeming Africa in the nineteenth century, in settling black people in a place where they would be free to exercise their talents.[55] Cuffe and Delany, like Garvey, were also interested in Africa for entrepreneurial reasons. Turner's zeal for emigration led him, toward the end of his career, to work with a group of white Alabama businessmen.[56] But Garveyism, unlike these earlier movements, was a twentieth-century recrudescence of colonization, whose chief actors were black rather than white. What made Garvey different from most nineteenth-century black pioneers of emigrationism was his acceptance of the fundamental premise of colonization: that is, black people had no future in the United States or Western world as free people and should return to Africa. This was not to be a total emigration; only the race-proud were to return to Africa.

> We do not want all the Negroes in Africa. Some are no good here, and naturally will be no good there. The no-good Negro will naturally die in fifty years. The Negro who is wrangling about fighting for social equality will naturally pass away in fifty years, and yield his place to the progressive Negro who wants a society and country of his own.[57]

Underlying Garvey's call for a return to Africa were certain ideas about race and history. These two combined were the centralizing vehicles of Garveyism—that is, its myth. Although Garvey could make statements like the following, they have to be measured against his attitudes toward mulattoes: "In twentieth century civilization there are no inferior and superior races."[58] "We desire to have every shade of colour, even those with one drop of African blood in our fold; because we believe that none of us, as we are, is responsible for our birth. In short we have no prejudice within the race. . . ."[59] These noble sentiments must be compared to the following statements about purity of race and mulattoes: "I believe in a pure black race just as how all self-respecting whites believe in a pure white race, as far as that can be." "Slavery brought upon us the curse of many colors within the Negro race." Mulattoes were evil and in the future the Negro race should not "be stigmatized by bastardy. . . ."[60]

Africa was important in Garvey's scheme because it would provide a haven for his abused race and because, he thought, a world without a Negro nation was a world destined to be torn apart by racial warfare. At the heart of Garvey's plan was a belief similar to that expressed by his great antagonist, W.E.B. DuBois, in his 1903 essay, "On the Dawn of Freedom." DuBois began the essay with these prophetic words: "The problem of the twentieth century is the problem of the color-line—the relation of the darker to the lighter races of men in Asia and Africa, in America and the islands of the sea."[61] Garvey, working independently of DuBois, arrived at a similar conclusion.

Garvey understood the pivotal importance of the Great War and saw the breakdown of pre-war European civilization as a time for concerted black assertion. What gave him hope was that other peoples were also asserting themselves as nationalities.

> The War of 1914–18 has created a new sentiment throughout the world. Once upon a time weaker peoples were afraid of expressing themselves, of giving vent to their feelings, but today no oppressed race or nation is afraid of speaking out in the cause of liberty. Egypt has spoken, Ireland has spoken, Poland has spoken and

> Poland is free, Ireland is also free. Africa is now speaking, and if for seven hundred and fifty years Irishmen found perseverance enough to have carried the cause of freedom on and on until they won, then four hundred million Negroes are prepared to carry on the fight for African liberty. . . .[62]

The world would only have peace after "a great inter-racial conference [was] called." To further facilitate the process of world peace Europeans should withdraw from Africa. For "Africa in the future [would] be to them what Europe [had] been for the last three hundred years—a hotbed of wars, political intrigues and upheavals."[63]

Underlying this rhetoric of doom and destruction was the belief that the "Negro must have a country of his own."[64] What blacks throughout the world wanted was "an independent African nationality."[65] The reason black people needed what Garvey called an "imperial whole" was that they were unprotected and victimized.[66] Nationhood would enable the Negro to make his place in the world like "other men." Because the black man was "made of the same physical and spiritual stuff that other men [were] made of," he needed a nation. "His position must not be inferior, but at least equal to that of others. To gauge the standard of equality, we have before us the deeds of other men."[67]

In some ways, Garvey's call for the creation of a black nation in Africa echoed Theodore Herzl's call for a Jewish state in Palestine.[68] Both men were skillful propagandists in pursuit of their goals. They also seem to have been oblivious or indifferent to the fact that the places where they wanted to establish their respective cities on the hill were already inhabited by people who did not share their vision. At the heart of Garvey and Herzl's dream was an attempt to refashion their people. They wanted to create for the "Lord's despised few" a new image—a national character that was essentially heroic: in short, a new identity.[69] Herzl thought that this would win his people "respect in the eyes of the world."[70] Garvey, proceeding along similar lines, created a flag and other accessory symbols of nationhood: a national anthem, a navy, Royal African Guards, an African Legion, Black Cross Nurses, a nobility, the Negro Factories Corporation, and a government in exile. Both Herzl's and Garvey's nationalism were rooted in modern notions of the nation state developed in the eighteenth century.[71] In addition, Garvey's nationalism in particular was essentially *volkish*, a return to a primitive tribalism in which membership in the group or nation was based on purity of blood. This can be most clearly seen in the conflicts that developed in the American black community after Garvey's arrival.

Commenting on his initial success, Garvey noted "what was impossible in Jamaica became immediately possible in the United States. . . ."[72] What made Garvey successful at first in America was the deteriorating state of race relations there. "Deterioration" is really the wrong word, for it connotes decline, and race relations were not declining, they were in their normal state, that is, bad. But the mob violence and the return to business as usual after the temporary improvement of the war years had heightened the dissatisfaction of black people — both north and south, native and alien. Garvey was able to capitalize on this when articulating his program of racial redemption.

He did this through a politics that was largely theatrical. Garvey was a master of what George Steiner has called "fantastication." Within a short time, he had made his presence known throughout black America by staging elaborate parades and court tableaux at Liberty Hall in Harlem.[73] These presentations bedazzled spectators; and for those black Americans and West Indians who were disposed to watch and listen, Garvey evoked images of a glorious Negro past and future.[74] Both the purpose and nature of these presentations raise questions about their being expressions of American Negro pride, as some historians have suggested.[75] On one level, Garvey's show was nothing more than a continuation of Booker T. Washington's "toothbrush" lessons. His wife makes this clear in her discussion of a reception held in 1921, "the main purpose of which was to train and demonstrate a better social behavior than formerly" existed within the race. No point of social decorum was left unattended. Invitees were even shown how to answer invitations. (This lesson was not learned by all—one R.S.V.P. read "D.S.C.C.," short for "dam sorry can't come.")[76] In her memoir of her husband's career, Mrs. Garvey described the reception in rhapsodic terms.

> The Hall was transformed into a magnificent tropical setting, with lighting effects, appropriate music being played. Each Dignitary was timed to arrive according to his rank, and an anthem or appropriate music played until he was seated. Potentate Johnson—resplendent in his uniform—inspected the Guard of Honour. Young Ladies were presented, and honours conferred on persons who had served the Race faithfully and well. Titles were: Knight Commander of the Nile, Distinguished Service Order of Ethiopia, and the Star of African Redemption. After the ceremonies, supper was served; guests were seated according to rank. Then followed the grand Ball, with all the courtliness of training, natural gift for dancing and love of music.[77]

This function and others that Garvey staged in Harlem illustrate his transferral of West Indian cultural sensibilities to the United States. Garvey's cultural tastes were those of a lower middle-class colonial who, having failed to make it in his own homeland, had moved his program to greener pastures. This, then, was Afro-British nationalism as described by Harold Cruse, "functioning outside its historical British context." At a time when Harlem was alive with the creative spirit of its renaissance, Garvey chose to ignore this cultural efflorescence. Bessie Smith, Ma Rainey, Ferdinand "Jelly Roll" Morton, and other popular American black entertainers did not make it to the stage of Liberty Hall. The musical fare heard at meetings in the Hall was limited to the light classics. On one occasion, for example, the musical selections included: "Ethel Clarke, Soprano, singing Eckert's Swiss song, and Cavallo's Chanson Mimi; The Black Star Line Band, in smart uniforms, rendering Overature [*sic*] from Rigoletto and Mirello; New York Local Choir, fully robed, singing the Bridal Chorus from the Rose Maiden and 'Gloria' from Mozart's 12th Mass; The 'Perfect Harmony Four' in Sextette from 'Lucia'; Basso Packer Ramsay sang Handel's 'Hear me ye Winds and Waves.'"[78]

If the Garvey movement was an expression of American black

nationalism—or black nationalism at all, for that matter—the symbols it used to express black pride were European, not African or African-American. Garvey's Royal African Guards, African Legion, and Black Cross Nurses may have evoked pride among Garvey's followers, but pride is only one level of consciousness. What did these uniforms do for the uninitiated? If a uniform is an egalitarian symbol, it also can be a highly elitist one, which separates the initiated from the uninitiated.[79] Garvey's creation of these uniformed phalanxes may also have created feelings of inadequacy among the non-adhering. Indeed, Garvey's adoption of these modes of dress and use of titles such as Duke, Knight Commander of the Sublime Order of the Nile, and Lady Commander of the Sublime Order of the Nile indicate that on the level of the subconscious he identified with the colonial oppressors of his people.[80]

Although he claimed to be liberating black people from centuries of oppression, his mode of liberation was identification with the oppressor/aggressor. The Garveyan alternative was not one of transcendence but one of engagement. This is what I meant earlier by the replication of culture. Even Garvey's support for the creation of an African Orthodox Church was nothing more than an acceptance of a Eurocentric form of Christianity. There were no "ring shouts" or "speaking in tongues" in the Garvey-sponsored Church.[81] Certainly if Garvey had been a connoisseur of Afro-American culture he would have seen in the American black church, particularly the evangelical wing of the black church, a great repository of genuine black culture.

If Garvey had limited himself solely to the threatrics of nationhood, he might have survived as a cult figure. But Garvey was a megalomaniac, and his delusions were ultimately to lead to his downfall. His principal chimera was a desire to create a black state in Africa. American black leaders saw his proposal as diversionary and impractical. They could agree with Garvey that black people should be proud of their race and know that they had a glorious history, but an African Republic or Imperium was not part of their program.[82] A. Philip Randolph expressed the skepticism of American black leaders when he remarked that "if Garvey is seriously interested in establishing a Negro nation why doesn't he begin with Jamaica, West Indies?"[83]

To those black people who were willing to listen, Garvey said there was no hope in striving for social equality within the United States.[84] According to Garvey the delusion about the possibility of achieving social equality had been planted in the minds of the Negro masses by a group of "self-appointed leaders of the race."[85] These racial spokesmen were "selfish" and the "pets of some philanthropists of another race, to whom [they would] go and debase [their] race in the worst form, humiliate [their] own manhood and thereby win the sympathy of the great benefactor."[86]

It is difficult to tell whether Garvey is talking in this passage about Booker T. Washington or W.E.B. DuBois. It is interesting to note, however, that after arriving in the United States, Garvey had concluded that the "Wizard's" program of racial uplift was deficient:

> . . . the Sage of Tuskegee has passed off the stage of life and left behind a new problem—a problem that must be solved, not by the industrial leaders only, but by the political and military leaders as well.

> If Washington had lived he would have had to change his program. No leader can successfully lead this race of ours without giving an interpretation of the New Negro who does not seek industrial opportunity alone, but a political voice.[87]

Garvey saw the political voice of the Negro in the United States as weak, timid, and integrationist. He was unsparing in his criticisms of men like DuBois, A. Phillip Randolph, and Chandler Owen, whom he condemned as traitors and opportunists, and thus enemies of the race.

> The present day or "colored" intellectual is no less a liar and cunning thief than his illustrious teacher. His occidental collegiate training only fits him to be a rogue and vagabond, and a seeker after the easiest and best by following the line of least resistance. He

is lazy, dull and uncreative. His purpose is to deceive the less fortunate of his race, and, by his wiles ride easily into position and wealth at their expense, and thereafter agitate for and seek social equality with creative and industrious whites.[88]

Garvey's detestation of these men grew by leaps and bounds as the 1920s unfolded and they became critical of his program of African redemption.

Garvey's attack on the established black leadership, especially DuBois, has traditionally been seen as a battle between classes, personalities, and ideologies. I would now like to suggest that it was also a race war, an intraracial struggle. In attacking DuBois and the other mulatto black spokesmen in the United States, Garvey introduced a new element into Afro-American politics. As Jervis Anderson has written, Garvey tried to read "light-skinned Negroes" out of the black race.[89] To Garvey, these people were the American embodiment of the Jamaican coloreds, diseased mongrels who hated themselves and their race. Garvey felt vindicated in this belief when DuBois referred to him in an article as a "little, fat, black man, ugly, but with intelligent eyes and a big head."[90] DuBois, a mulatto of French Huguenot, Dutch, and black ancestry, was described in turn by Garvey as a racial "monstrosity."[91] To Garvey, mixed ancestry was a sign of racial degeneration. In taking this position, he followed the path laid out by Edward Wilmot Blyden, the great Pan-African patriot of the nineteenth and early twentieth centuries.[92] Blyden, like Garvey, hated mulattoes and called them "mongrels," "vipers," "degenerates," and "deceivers." Following the ideas of the physiologist Dr. Joseph Henry, Blyden thought that "the ideas of a people depended largely upon blood. If there [was] blood degeneration, there [would] be thought degeneration."[93] This is what Garvey meant when he called DuBois a "monstrosity": that because DuBois was of mixed parentage his racial sensibilities were confused. He was easily seduced by the blandishments of whites because his sense of racial pride had been attenuated by blood degeneration.[94] Confused by the reality of race, Garvey maintained, DuBois and his followers continued to be trapped in the false promise of social equality, a cruel hoax because the basic problem between black and white was economic.

> When white men are faced with unemployment and apparent hunger and starvation, they have no respect for law, if the law stands in the way of their finding work and bread. Every un-employed white man looks upon the Negro as a dangerous com-petitor for possible employment, and in that case he loses all reason and respect for law and will go to any extent, even that of scaring and lynching the Negro so as to keep him away from the possibility of getting the job he wants.[95]

When you strip away all of the high-flown rhetoric, Garvey's analysis of the race problem was expressed essentially in economic terms. This does not mean that he was a Marxist. On the contrary, Garvey was a dyed-in-the-wool capitalist. "Capitalism is neces-sary to the progress of the world," he said, "and those who un-reasonably and wantonly oppose or fight against it are enemies to human advancement. . . ."[96] Garvey's belief in free enterprise made him hostile to socialists, communists, and trade unionists — who he claimed made up "99 1/2 percent" of lynch mobs.[97] Far from advocating black membership in trade unions, Garvey ad-vised black workers to organize by themselves and to keep their wages lower than whites. This, he said, would earn the Negro worker "the good will" of their white employers.[98] Whether this strategy reflected Garvey's earlier experience with unions is diffi-cult to say. What is quite clear, though, is that he had a deep and abiding suspicion of whites, especially those who were interested in helping the race.

> The greatest enemies of the Negro are among those who hypo-critically profess love and fellowship for him, when, in truth, and deep down in their hearts, they despise and hate him. Pseudo-philanthropists and their organizations are killing the Negro. White men and women of the Morefield Storey, Joel Spingarn, Julius Rosenwald, Oswald Garrison Villard, Congressman Dyer and Mary White Ovington type, in conjunction with the above-mentioned agencies, are disarming, dis-visioning, dis-ambitioning and fooling the Negro to death. They teach the Negro to look to the whites in a

false direction. They, by their practices, are endeavoring to hold the Negroes in check, as a possible dangerous minority group, and yet point them to the impossible dream of equality that shall never materialize, as they well know, and never intended; at the same time distracting the Negro from the real solution and objective of securing nationalism. By thus decoying and deceiving the Negro and side-tracking his real objective, they hope to gain time against him in allowing others of their race to perfect the plan by which the blacks are to be completely destroyed as a competitive permanent part of white majority civilization and culture. They have succeeded in enslaving the ignorance of a small group of so-called "Negro intellectuals" whom they use as agents to rope in the unsuspicious colored or Negro people.[99]

DuBois and his white friends in the NAACP, like "an earlier group that fooled the Negro during the days of Reconstruction," were enemies of the race, according to Garvey. Instead of encouraging the Negro to leave America, "as Jefferson and Lincoln did, they sought to revenge him in the white man's civilization; to further rob his labor, and exploit his ignorance, until he [was] subsequently ground to death by a newly developed superior white civilization."[100]

But if the NAACP was an enemy of the race, Garvey thought, the Negro nevertheless had friends in America. Like the blacks themselves, these friends were also victimized, persecuted, and harassed, because they spoke a truth which the race's enemies found unpalatable. Garvey's call for black emigration to Africa was endorsed by the Ku Klux Klan and the Anglo-Saxon Clubs, two racist organizations flourishing in postwar America. In Garvey, the Klan and Anglo-Saxon Clubs found an answer to their prayers. Major Earnest Sevier Cox, the author of the racist tract *White America*, called Garvey " a martyr for the independence and integrity of the Negro race."[101] Garvey was equally admiring of Cox and John Powell, the organizer of the Anglo-Saxon Clubs. These men were honest, Garvey thought, and reflected the true racial sensibilities of white America.

Between the Ku Klux Klan and the Morefield Storey National Association for the Advancement of "Colored" People group, give me
the Klan for their honesty of purpose towards the Negro. They are
better friends to my race, for telling us what they are, and what they
mean, thereby giving us a chance to stir for ourselves, than all the
hypocrites put together with their false gods and religions, not with-
standing. You may call me a Klansman if you will, but, potentially,
every white man is a Klansman, as far as the Negro in competition
with whites socially, economically and politically is concerned, and
there is no use lying about it.[102]

Garvey's association with these white supremacists and his en-
dorsement of their ideas was a reflection of the basic racist and
reactionary nature of his movement. His attack on DuBois and
other American black spokesmen was an attempt to turn back the
racial clock in America. To be sure, this clock was moving slowly,
but it was moving.

In attempting to subdivide the race along racial lines, Garvey
revealed his ignorance of American racial mores, on the one hand,
and on the other hand demonstrated a great psychological bold-
ness. In an age of mass politics, in which ordinary people felt
deracinated, Garvey appealed to a primordial sensibility—blood.
If he had succeeded, the results for black people in the United
States would have been disastrous. Writing in the *New York Am-
sterdam News* on June 12, 1937, A.M. Wendell Malliet spelled out
the sinister implications of the Garvey movement when he wrote:
"Garvey's bold and spectacular leadership would have created a
situation in Harlem and Negro America like that which has developed in Germany under Hitler. Garveyism would have em-
boldened the mob and engendered intraracial and interracial strife.
Garvey's personal leadership would have encouraged the masses
to take things in their own hands whenever a situation was sufficiently provoking—if Garvey were in Harlem today."[103]

Was Garvey a fascist? The answer is no. However, his ideology
contained certain proto-fascist elements, which can be seen in the
emphasis Garvey placed on the masses, in his hostility to communism and socialism, in the pan-nationalist pretensions of the

UNIA, and above all in the stress placed on purity of blood.[104]
The Garvey movement is best understood as an effort to reorder
the world for black people. In this sense Garvey was a forerunner
of Hitler and Mussolini, who also tried to make the world a better
place for their people. Garvey did not, in my estimation, offer
black people "a concrete and appealing alternative," as one scholar
has recently claimed.[105] Nor did his movement mean, as Professor
Hill has recently suggested, "the freeing of black men and women
from the cultural domination of Europe, from the cultural and
psychological domination of whiteness."[106] What then did Garvey offer the world and black people? "It was an essentially un-
serious world," as Dennis Mack Smith has recently written of Italy
under Mussolini, "where prestige, propaganda, and public statements were what counted; and it is hard to avoid the conclusion that
this was the central message and real soft core at the heart of Italian
fascism."[107] Garvey, like Mussolini, was a virtuoso illusionist.

Massa's New Clothes: A Critique of
Eugene D. Genovese on Southern Society,
Master-Slave Relations, and Slave Behavior

Since Kenneth Stampp published his magisterial *The Peculiar Institution*, American historians have been in search of a paradigm that would explain southern society, master-slave relations, and slave behavior in the antebellum South.[1] A recent effort in this quest is Eugene D. Genovese's *Roll, Jordan, Roll.*

In his books and articles Professor Genovese has established himself as a perceptive and learned student of the antebellum South and American Negro slavery.[2] All of his work, though, has been conceptualized around one idea—the idea of hegemony, which Genovese borrowed from the work of Antonio Gramsci.[3] Gwyn Williams summarizes Gramsci's thought in this way:

> By "hegemony" Gramsci seems to mean a sociopolitical situation, in his terminology a "moment," in which the philosophy and practice of a society fuse or are in equilibrium; an order in which a certain way of life and thought is dominant, in which one concept of reality is diffused throughout society in all its institutional and private manifestations, informing with its spirit all taste, morality, customs, religious and political principles, and all social relations, particularly in their intellectual and moral connotation.[4]

Some scholars might find hegemony to be a useful concept for the study of southern society, master-slave relations, and slave behavior. But Genovese's use of Gramsci's concept is open to criticism because he employs it in such a way as to fit any relationship and form of behavior into his neo-Gramscian framework. In *The Political Economy of Slavery* he asserts:

> The premodern quality of the Southern world was imparted to it by its dominant slaveholding class. . . . The plantation society that had begun as an appendage of British capitalism ended as a powerful, largely autonomous civilization. . . . The essential element in this distinct civilization was the slaveholders' domination. . . . The planters commanded Southern politics and set the tone of social life. Theirs was an aristocratic, antibourgeois spirit.[5]

What Genovese presents here is a series of assertions, not a structured analytical system. His statements, for example, that the "planters commanded Southern politics" and were "antibourgeois [in] spirit" are questionable, and these problems will be dealt with later on. All that need be noted here is that these difficulties are related to his use of the notion of hegemony. As Genovese uses it, the concept obscures more than it reveals. Genovese has taken U.B. Phillips's analysis of the paternalistic slave system and given it Marxian clothing.[6]

In producing this new habiliment he tailors the evidence to fit the model. What emerges from his work is a logical and coherent history of southern society, master-slave relations, and slave behavior. Logic is the great virtue of the concept of hegemony, and this perhaps is why Genovese has used it to study slavery. Hegemony provides him with a social model into which events and people can be fitted in such a way as to make all of their actions comprehensible. It enables Genovese to argue that a complex social system was integrated by shared values. Thus, Genovese can say that southern society "bound two peoples together in bitter antagonism while creating an organic relationship so complex and ambivalent that neither could express the simplest human feelings without reference to the other."[7] Furthermore, he can assert that masters and slaves were linked by a paternalism based "upon mutual obligations — duties, responsibilities, and ultimately even rights — [which] recognized the slaves' humanity."[8] Hegemony allows Genovese to preserve his belief in class domination and yet explain the lack of actual, visible class conflict. When viewed in this context, the notion of hegemony becomes part of a long and continuing Marxist effort to explain why the great revolutions did not occur as they were supposed to. Stated briefly, hegemony is supposed to tell us why there were no successful slave revolts in the United States. This problem in Genovese's analysis will be dealt with below. Finally, hegemony permits Genovese to engage in a fashionable discussion of culture and make the equally fashionable point that the slaves developed a culture of their own. Taken as a whole, this history is too logical to be an accurate picture of the past, for what Genovese has done is to take an ambiguous theoretical construct and make it precise. In brief, Genovese's hegemony coheres where Gramsci's may not have, for Gramsci's writings suggest that a ruling class's exercise of hegemony was never total nor static. Furthermore, hegemony's scope and impact, Gramsci argued, varied from one society to another.[9] Genovese makes only perfunctory obeisance to these qualifications. Hegemony as he uses the concept is all encompassing and pervasive.

When applied to the antebellum South, hegemony suggests that nonelite groups (nonslaveholders and slaves) accepted the overlordship of the planter aristocracy, and, moreover, that the planter's ideology pervaded southern society in such a way, as Genovese says, "to convince the lower classes that its interests [were] those of the society at large."[10] This idea is difficult to sustain, and Genovese's defense of it is not successful. Hegemony, then, as a paradigm used by Genovese, can only be applied to the slave South if it is qualified, and these qualifications undermine its applicability.

Nonslaveholders: The Problem of Hegemony

Genovese's argument that the planters exercised a hegemony over the nonslaveholders is not supported by the evidence. At various times in the history of the South the nonslaveholders found themselves at odds with the planters. As several historians have shown, these differences of opinion involved disputes over political representation, taxes, and the peculiar institution itself.[11] Indeed, what these scholars suggest is that the planter's dominance was never so absolute as to constitute a "hegemony."

To resolve this problem, Genovese has recently tried to refine his interpretation of southern society — stumbling once again over hegemony. The term, as Genovese uses it, assumes universal socialization. In the antebellum South this meant that the planters' *Weltanschauung* was internalized by the nonslaveholding whites and became "common sense knowledge."[12] Taken literally this assumption rules out the possibility of the nonslaveholders developing an alternative world view. Genovese is too clever to adopt this position totally, and, in an essay published after the appearance of *Roll, Jordan, Roll*, he criticizes historians who have suggested that the nonslaveholders were supine and ideologically controlled by the planter aristocracy. After commenting on the limitations of this explanation and the deficiencies of "Herrenvolk Democracy" as a conceptual framework for the study of the nonslaveholders' allegiance to the South, Genovese posits a new way of looking at this problem.[13]

According to Genovese the planters and nonslaveholders were bound "together by links firm enough to account for the political unity of the South; it was precisely the conjecture of these economic, political, and cultural forces, including intense racism, that made secession and sustained warfare possible."[14] The rest of the article is devoted to demonstrating the validity of these propositions. Readers familiar with Genovese's work might expect that this essay would represent a refinement of his use of the hegemonic paradigm or even put forth a recognition that the nonslaveholders possessed a world view of their own. However, this shift in emphasis is more cosmetic than real. Consider the following paragraphs:

> In short, so long as the yeomen accepted the existing master-slave relationship as either something to aspire to or something peripheral to their own lives, they were led step-by-step into willing acceptance of a subordinate position in society. They accepted that

position not because they did not understand their interest, nor because they were panicked by racial fears, and certainly not because they were stupid, but because they saw themselves as aspiring slaveholders or as nonslaveholding beneficiaries of a slaveholding world, the only world they knew. To have considered their position in any other terms would have required a herculean effort and a degree of sophistication capable of penetrating the indirect and subtle workings of the system as a whole. . . .

It was not impossible that ordinary farmers could have accomplished that herculean effort and attained that sophistication. The secession crisis and especially the defection from the Confederacy demonstrated the fragility of the up-country's loyalty to the regime. And even in the plantation belt, the slaveholders were by no means sure that arguments as that of Hinton Helper would not take hold among a basically literate, politically experienced, and fiercely proud white population, if economic conditions deteriorated or free discussion was encouraged. The slaveholders contained the threat by preventing the message from reaching the people—by placing the slavery question beyond discussion. It did not, however, require a genius to recognize that a hostile free soil regime in Washington, the constant agitation of the slavery question within the national Union, or some internal crisis that upset the delicate ideological balance within the South might lead to the emergence of an antislavery movement at home. Secession and independence had much to recommend them to the dominant propertyholders of so dangerous a world.[15]

Just what is Genovese saying? Is he arguing that the nonslaveholders did not suffer from false consciousness and derived more than vicarious satisfaction from being members of a slaveholding world? If this is so then why was Hinton Helper's book *The Impending Crisis* such a threat to this well-reasoned and ideologically balanced system? What prevented these rational nonslaveholders from recognizing their interest? Why was it that Helper's book could not be seen as a piece of Republican propaganda and therefore dismissed as such?[16] The big question here is why secession? As described by Genovese, the nonslaveholders posed no threat to the peculiar institution or the planter's hegemony. Just what, then, is the internal threat that the planters "contain" when they secede? If "secession and independence had much to recommend them," they also suggested caution, as the history of the Confederacy makes clear.[17]

Genovese is also on dubious ground when he asserts that the nonslaveholders "were not panicked by racial fears," for racial fears in the South cut across class lines and affected slaveholders and nonslaveholders alike. This was particularly true after 1826 when dozens of laws were passed to protect white men and their families from what William W. Freehling has called "a disturbing institution."[18] There were widespread slave insurrection panics in 1831, 1834, 1856, 1859, and 1860. After each of these incidents the white South was gripped by hysteria, and many innocent blacks were killed because of white racial fears.[19] Even in times of racial peace, planters and nonslaveholders manifested anxiety about slavery, unless we assume that the slave patrols and vigilance committees reflect a society at peace with itself.

The Slaves: The Problem of Paternalism

The major problem with Genovese's use of the concept of paternalism is the thinness of his evidence. Genovese's argument that the planters were paternalistic rests largely on a series of assertions and on the writings of George Fitzhugh.[20] Genovese realizes that Fitzhugh was not representative of southern thought, but nevertheless he was "a ruthless and critical theorist who spelled out the logical outcome of the slaveholder's philosophy and laid bare its essence."[21] Unfortunately for both Genovese and Fitzhugh, recent scholarship suggests that Fitzhugh was a peripheral figure in the defense of slavery. Some of his contemporaries indeed feared that Fitzhugh's work would lead northerners to believe all southerners were fanatics.[22] But in terms of Genovese's analysis of southern society Fitzhugh is a central figure, for, without Fitzhugh, he cannot claim that the South was prebourgeois or antimaterialistic. Genovese's use of Fitzhugh is a classic example of selecting evidence to sustain an *a priori* conclusion. Drew Faust makes this point clearly when she writes that "Genovese's analysis of Fitzhugh is ultimately circular, for it defines the South as prebourgeois and then embraces the single Southerner who openly attacked capitalism as the most accurate exponent of the regional world view."[23] These problems also carry over into Genovese's analysis of the world the slaves made.

Genovese begins his discussion of antebellum slavery by asserting that "slavery bound two peoples together in bitter antagonism while creating an organic relationship so complex and ambivalent that neither could express the simplest human feelings without reference to the other."[24] To sustain this generalization, Genovese draws on a variety of materials: diaries, journals, songs and oral traditions, all of these items taken from different times and places in the history of the Old South. They give *Roll, Jordan, Roll* a rich texture and make it, at least in places, an exciting book to read. Excitement, though, obscures the monograph's major flaw — a static portrait of slavery. Although *Roll, Jordan, Roll* is subtitled "The World the Slaves Made," the process central to the creation of this world is absent from its pages. "Culture is not a fixed condition but a process," as Lawrence W. Levine has written; it is "the product of interaction between past and present."[25] If Genovese had begun his discussion of slave culture in the seventeenth century and traced the world the slaves made through time, that is, chronicled its evolution in the eighteenth century and first six decades of the nineteenth century, his treatment of slave culture would be more complete, and readers of *Roll, Jordan, Roll* would be able to see how slave culture changed over time. Tracing the interaction between past and present would have enabled Genovese to show both continuities and disjunctures in slave culture. Since culture is not a static phenomenon, each generation of slaves received a cultural heritage that it either added to or modified and then passed on to its progeny. One wonders, then, if a more appropriate subtitle for *Roll, Jordan, Roll* might not be, the *worlds* the slaves made.[26] This would take into account cultural changes between and within generations of slaves.

Furthermore, an analysis focusing on the issue of cultural change between and within generations of bondspeople would illuminate another problem in Genovese's work, his use of the term *paternalism*. Genovese employs "paternalism" as an umbrella under which all master-slave relations are subsumed. It would be interesting if Genovese could show how the paternalistic ideology evolved over time and whether or not it changed according to circumstances. Stated another way—was the response of each generation of slaves the same to paternalism or were some generations more restive than others? Answering this question would elucidate an observation about the nature of social history that Genovese and his wife, Elizabeth Fox-Genovese, have recently made. "History," the Genoveses say, "when it transcends chronicle, romance and ideology—including left wing versions—is primarily the story of who rides whom and how."[27] In *Roll, Jordan, Roll* the concept of paternalism explains "how" the slaves were ridden. But does it? For paternalism, as Genovese defines it, emphasizes the mutual or reciprocal nature of master-slave relations.[28] The same kind of relations exist between sadist and masochist and executioners and their victims. In short, most relations between human beings involve some form of exchange. The major problem with this definition, though, is that it downplays the coercive nature of slavery.

Plantation slavery in the period that Genovese discusses did not involve either mutuality or reciprocity. In short, it was not paternalistic. The planters may have defended slavery with a rhetoric whose imagery was domestic and familial, but this was only a smokescreen for exploitation or a technique of exploitation. A desire for profits produced a need for efficient laborers, which meant that the slaves had to work as a unit.[29] Frederick Law Olmsted understood this when he wrote "the treatment of the mass must be reduced to a system, the ruling idea of which will be, to enable one man to force into the same channel of labor the muscles of a large number of men, of various, and often conflicting wills."[30] Plantation life was accompanied by a great deal of cruelty. Slaves were punished for not working efficiently, as the diary of Bennet Barrow makes clear.[31] Barrow was not just a "harsh master," as Genovese claims. Barrow was a sadist who on one occasion called his punishment of slaves a "whipping frolic."[32] Barrow's behavior suggests that some planters derived more than financial rewards from their management of their bondservants.

Even if the plantations were paternalistic enterprises, the question must be asked if this form of social organization represented an advance over the institutions of the North that George Fitzhugh denounced.[33] The answer is no. The fact that planters included slaves in their family circles should not, as Genovese suggests, lead one to believe that slavery was paternalistic. Indeed, a great deal of the system's injustice occurred in the familial context, as Gerald Mullin has suggested in *Flight and Rebellion*.[34] Harriet Beecher Stowe made this same point earlier in her novel *Uncle Tom's Cabin*.[35] Stowe depicted the suffering of Tom and other slaves who were privileged members of their masters' households to indicate that paternalism was no protection from the cruelty inherent in the slave system. As the narratives of Solomon Northrup, Austin Steward, and George Brown make clear, slavery was no hayride.[36] Moreover, as long as slaves, even privileged ones, were perceived as children, their humanity was denied. This denial of humanity was reinforced when the planters called their favorites "auntie," "uncle," and "boy." Rather than connoting familial affection these terms only emphasized the slaves' powerlessness. Genovese ignored this in his effort "to tell the story of slave life as carefully and accurately as possible."[37] What Genovese actually has done is deemphasize race.

Color, Physiognomy, Race: The Problem of Class

Questions of race and racial purity troubled antebellum white Americans, as a number of studies of racial attitudes in this period have shown.[38] It is interesting therefore to see an analysis of slavery that conflates race and class. Slavery, Genovese says:

By definition and in essence . . . was a system of class rule, in which some people lived off the labor of others. American slavery subordinated one race to another and thereby rendered its fundamental class relationships more complex and ambiguous; but they remained class relationships.[39]

This is an interesting generalization, but it does not take into account the role that color and race played in shaping antebellum American racial sensibilities. The two (color and race) bound all black people in North America together. They were in the eyes of whites, North and South, "colored people." "Slavery," as Carl Degler has noted, "had [a] homogenizing effect only in the United States. In every other slave society in the new world, a clear and important social distinction was made between free blacks and free mulattoes, that is, between people of different skin color or appearance."[40] Genovese is correct, therefore, when he states that slavery was a form of subordination, but this statement does not go far enough. It ignores the fact that slavery was a form of racial rather than class distinction and oppression.[41] But denoting slavery as a form of class rule creates other problems, which relate to context and perception.

In the context of antebellum society, only blacks were slaves. Both whites and blacks knew this, and it affected their inter- and intrapersonal relations. What seems to have been primary in these relations was color and physiognomy. The constant references in proslavery literature to the Negroes' apelike appearance, woolly hair, and thick lips indicate how important these characteristics were to white southerners in differentiating themselves from blacks, whether free or slave.[42] The following comments by William L. Yancey on the repeal of a Massachusetts law prohibiting interracial marriage illustrate this point:

. . . the black son of Africa, with flat nose, thick lips, protruding [c]hin, and skin redolent of rare odors. Although purportedly free to compete on equal terms with the white man to ally himself with, ay, and even [be] invited to the arms of, the fair-skinned[,] cherry-lipped, and graceful daughter of that famed [Puritan] race, [he] still retains his nature — rejects with scorn the tendered connection, and prefers to revel in the brothel, until imprisoned in jail or penitentiary.[43]

And speaking in another context, William H. Roane of Virginia used similar language to describe Negroes: "I no more believe that the flat-nosed, wooly haired black native of the deserts of Africa, is equal to the straight-haired white man of Europe, than I believe the stupid, scentless grey-haired hound is equal to the noble, generous dog of Newfoundland."[44] What these quotations reveal is the general nineteenth-century white fear of miscegenation, a fear that was also associated with a dread of loss of sexual and social control.[45] In Genovese's analysis of slavery, the question of race and the phobias that whites expressed on this subject are not dealt with. Master-slave relations are interpreted solely in terms of class relations. But is this the way antebellum white men viewed this problem? The evidence suggests that it was not.

The web of proscription that black people, slave and free, lived in shows that they were not perceived by whites as just another class. In making this argument it is not my intention to deny that the slaves were a class. This is obvious. But, as a class in antebellum society, slaves and free blacks, because of their color, were forced to relate to white people in ways that set them apart from other groups in American society. As Robert Blauner has observed,

> Racist social relations have different cultural consequences from class relations and therefore . . . cannot be forced into the procrustean bed of lower-class culture. . . . Racism excludes a category of people from participation in society in a different way than does class hegemony and exploitation. The thrust of racism is to dehumanize, to violate dignity and degrade personalities in a much more pervasive and all-inclusive way than class exploitation — which in the United States, at any rate, has typically not been generalized beyond the point of production. For these reasons, racial and class oppression — while intimately interacting — have diverse consequences for group formation, for the salience of identities based upon them, and for individual and group modes of adaptation and resistance.[46]

In *Roll, Jordan, Roll* Genovese conflates race and class and in doing so vitiates his assertion that slavery was "a class relationship." For if slavery was a class relationship then why were only Negroes slaves? Why, for example, were not the Irish enslaved when they entered antebellum America? As a group the Irish were caricatured and stereotyped in the same manner blacks were. The Irish were said to be dirty, lazy, sexually promiscuous, drunken, riotous, and also apelike in their appearance. Despite this perception, the Irish were not enslaved, because they were white. Although possessing both cultural and physical characteristics that Anglo Saxon Protestants found distasteful, color permitted the Irish eventually to become a part of the country's dominant group.[47] By downplaying the importance of color, physiognomy, and race in the nineteenth century, Genovese obscures the core of antebellum racism. In short, Negroes were slaves because they were defenseless and *black*, not because they were a class in the Marxian sense, as Genovese uses the term.[48]

Unlike Genovese, the supreme courts of Arkansas and Delaware recognized the racial nature of American slavery when they ruled that free blacks could not own other blacks. In Arkansas the court held:

> . . . slavery . . . has its foundation in an inferiority of race. There is a striking difference between the black and white man, in intellect, feelings and principles. In the order of providence, the former was made inferior to the latter; and hence the bondage of the one to the other. . . . The bondage of one negro to another, has not this solid foundation to rest upon. The free negro finds in the slave his brother in blood, in color, feelings, education and principle. He has but few civil rights, nor can have, consistent with the good order of society; . . . civilly and morally disqualified to extend protection, and exercise dominion over the slave.[49]

Delaware's court followed a similar line of reasoning when it denied free blacks the privilege deemed suitable only for whites.

> . . . we observe one . . . pervading feature [of slavery], that the black is the slave to the white man; . . . this court . . . will not extend slavery beyond what it has been heretofore, . . . to give the free negro a right to hold slaves, would be to institute another and a dangerous species of slavery hitherto unknown . . . the negro is not such a freeman as to extend protection; he is . . . almost as helpless

and dependent on the white race as the slave himself; . . . We think, therefore, that neither usage, policy, nor the necessary relations of master and slave, will permit free negroes in this state to hold slaves.[50]

What these actions by the supreme courts of Arkansas and Delaware show is the racial nature of American Negro slavery. Although the rest of the southern states did not have laws like these on their books, most white southerners disapproved of blacks owning other blacks. A black slaveowner was an anomaly in a society where possession of black skin was a presumption of bondage.[51] Finally, widespread Negro ownership of slaves would have brought into question the racial basis of slavery, and this was a possibility that white southerners did not want to contemplate.

"The Rock and the Church": The Problem of Hegemony

Probably the most admired section of *Roll, Jordan, Roll* is Genovese's analysis of slave religion. Although Genovese's discussion of this aspect of the world the slaves made is wide ranging and learned, the overall examination is conducted within the framework of paternalism, which required mutual accommodations and obligations between master and slave.[52] The use of this conceptual scheme gives Genovese's interpretations of slave religion a curious twist. This is particularly true of his examination of the doctrine of original sin and millennialism.

Like several recent studies of slave religion, Genovese's analysis is largely functional.[53] Religion, he says, "was a weapon of defense" that taught the slaves "to love and value each other, to take a critical view of their masters, and to reject the ideological rationales for their own enslavement."[54] The insights learned from this process enabled the slaves to transcend the oppressive system that bound them to their masters. Religion provided the slaves with an alternative sense of community, and within this world of their own the slaves created styles of worship that reflected African and American religious sensibilities.[55]

To illustrate this point Genovese compares the religious experiences of Brazilian and American slaves. In Brazil religion had a double dimension: "It enabled [the slaves] to accommodate with some measure of cultural autonomy and personal dignity, and, more rarely but ominously, it provided the war cry for determined insurgents."[56] His examination of how the slaves worshipped in their quarters is one of the finest in the current literature on this subject.[57] But slave songs, styles of preaching, and shouts are secondary considerations in Genovese's study of how the bondspeople worshipped.[58] Genovese's functional emphasis stressed not religion itself, but how religion served as a catalyst for slave revolt. The religion of Brazilian slaves, Genovese argues, contained the seeds of both accommodation and rebellion.[59] In the United States this dichotomy was more heavily weighted toward accommodation. The explanation for this is the focus of Genovese's analysis of American slave religion. His central concern is politics, "who rides whom and how."[60] In *Roll, Jordan, Roll* the slaves' religion partially answers this question.[61]

The heart of Genovese's analysis is a curious argument about the doctrine of original sin and millennialism.[62] According to Genovese, a belief in original sin was not central to American slave Christianity. The slaves rejected this tenet for two reasons: first, because it was used to justify their bondage and, second, because the slaves' West African cultural heritage, although diluted, did not die. The religions of West Africa, Genovese says, "did not espouse a doctrine of original sin."[63] Therefore the slaves' conversion to Christianity did not "result in a full surrender to this most profound and fateful of Christian ideas."[64] Shaping Christianity to fit their own needs, the slaves fashioned a religion that was "life affirming." This Christianity "lacked that terrible inner tension between the sense of guilt and the sense of mission that once provided the ideological dynamism for Western civilization's march to world power."[65] What Genovese is saying here is that the religion of American slaves was not ascetic, for it "affirmed joy in life in the face of every trial." If the American slaves' religion had been more ascetic, Genovese seems to be arguing, they would have developed "a revolutionary or politically militant millennialism and messianism."[66] For asceticism "has provided a decisive ingredient in the mobilization of popular uprisings."[67]

Although interesting, these observations about original sin, millennialism, and asceticism tell us more about Genovese than they do about slave Christianity. For it is not clear, as the following examples indicate, that the religion of American slaves was devoid of these doctrines. The narratives of Richard Allen, Josiah Henson, J.W.C. Pennington, and William Heard show that the doctrine of original sin was important in their conversion to Christianity.[68] And how could it be otherwise, since the denominations that these black men joined placed great emphasis on a conversion experience? Any slave who wanted to become a Baptist, Methodist, or Presbyterian had to be born again. They had to recognize, as Richard Allen did in the throes of his conversion, that the "Saviour" had died for them.[69] To doubt this proposition or any other Christian doctrine was the "sin of sins."[70] Finally, the experiences of a Florida planter named Kingsley suggest that even a paternalistic slave owner could be ruined by a combination of asceticism, "a quietist version of millenialism," and a sense of sin.[71] Kingsley wrote:

> I never interfered in their connubial concerns nor domestic affairs, but let them regulate these after their own manner. I taught them nothing but what was useful, and what I thought would add to their physical and moral happiness. I encouraged as much as possible dancing, merriment and dress, for which Saturday afternoon and night and Sunday mornings were dedicated. (Part of their leisure) was usually employed in hoeing their corn and getting a supply of fish for the week. . . . Both men and women were very industrious. Many of them made twenty bushels of corn to sell, and they vied with each other in dress and dancing. . . . They were perfectly happy, having no fear but that of offending me; and I hardly ever had to apply other correction than shaming them. If I exceeded this the punishment was quite light, for they hardly ever failed in doing their work well. My object was to excite their ambition and attachment by kindness, not to depress their spirits by fear and punishment. . . . Perfect confidence, friendship and good understanding reigned between us.

During the war of 1812 most of these slaves were either killed or carried off by Seminoles. After the war, Kingsley began operations again, only to have his plantation Eden disrupted again.

> . . . a serpent entered in the guise of a Negro preacher who taught the sinfulness of dancing, fishing on Sunday and eating the catfish which had no scales. In consequence the slaves became poor, ragged, hungry and disconsolate. To steal from me was only to do justice—to take what belonged to them, because I kept them in unjust bondage. They came to believe that all pastime or pleasure in this iniquitous world was sinful; that this was only a place of sorrow and repentence, and the sooner they were out of it the better; that they would then go to a good country where they would experience no want of anything, and have no work nor cruel taskmaster for that God was merciful and would pardon any sin they committed; only it was necessary to pray and ask what they could to the church, etc. . . . Finally myself and the overseer became completely divested of all authority over the Negroes. . . . Severity had no effect; it only made it worse.[72]

What this incident shows is that the religion of American slaves did not have to be revolutionary or politically militant and messianic to be an effective force for resistance. Indeed the use of these categories for the analysis of slave Christianity obscures more than it reveals. For as Martin Marty has recently written, "very few [people] have used their spiritual sustenance only in order to organize for eventual revolution."[73] At some level Genovese may understand this point, but in order to sustain the hegemonic paradigm, he must raise the question of why American slaves did not revolt. In all fairness to Genovese, it must be said that he does indicate that there were other social and political circumstances that militated against a successful slave revolt in the United States.[74] However, in his presentation religion takes precedence over these, for, although life-affirming, it did not prevent some slaves from being fatalistic.[75] Moreover, because American slave Christianity lacked an ascetic thrust it seems to have made the slaves passive with respect to political action. And within the context of the hegemonic paradigm religion induced the slaves to *consent* to their own exploitation and misery.[76]

Consent is the key word here, for hegemony is a form of pre-dominance obtained by consent rather than force.[77] In Geno-vese's interpretation of American slave Christianity, religion is the vehicle of consent. Although life-affirming, the slaves' Chris-tianity did not generate a sense of denial (asceticism) that would culminate in revolt. Religion mystified the slaves' sense of politi-cal power and reconciled them to their position in society.[78]

Is this a plausible assessment of slave Christianity? Or is it an analysis designed to fit the hegemonic paradigm? By answering the second question we arrive at an answer to the first. Religion in Genovese's overall analysis of American slave culture is the only facet of slave life that could provide the slaves with an alter-native sensibility to the planters' paternalism. Because Genovese's thesis obliges him to treat the planters' power as pervasive, he must deny that the slaves had a world view that was independent of their masters' outlook.

The concept of hegemony is inadequate as a conceptual frame-work for the study of southern society, master-slave relations, and slave behavior. The framework obscures more than it reveals. It enables Genovese to present an interpretation that is at vari-ance, in its specifics, with the facts of history. He dresses U.B. Phillips's benevolent slave master in a new set of clothing. Unfor-tunately for both Genovese and Phillips, this new attire, like the emperor's, is an illusion.

Is an alternative framework possible? It may be, but nothing here should be construed as suggesting one. I agree with James Henretta's recent observation that "some philosophical positions and analytic strategies satisfy me more than others." I do not ac-cept Genovese's hegemonic framework. For, as a system of ex-planation, hegemony tells us more about the masters than the slaves.[79] Ultimately the question must be asked: what did the planters need hegemony for when they had guns?[80]

Black Reconstruction in America: W.E.B. DuBois's Challenge to "The Dark and Bloody Ground of Reconstruction Historiography"

"The Civil War," Robert Penn Warren has written, "is for the American imagination the great single event of our history."[1] But if the victory of the North in the Civil War represents America at its best, the Reconstruction which followed that heroic struggle has a less glorious aura. Until twenty years ago in both academic and popular circles Reconstruction represented excess, degeneration, and a deviation from the norms of Anglo-Saxon good government.[2] Beginning in the 1870s this viewpoint was disseminated by a disaffected Republican politician named James S. Pike. Like a number of nineteenth-century Republicans, Pike was no friend of the Negro. Thus, in 1873, when Pike published his book *The Prostrate State*, subtitled *South Carolina under Negro Government*, he did more than shed light, as Robert F. Durden claims, "on the ambiguities and the limitations that were an inherent part of the antislavery crusade and the Reconstruction program of the Republican party."[3] Pike also prefigured an important school of American historical interpretation which Kenneth Stampp has called the "Tragic Legend."[4] What exactly did Pike do?

Central to James S. Pike's analysis of Reconstruction was the idea that what had taken place was the Africanization of South Carolina under which, he claimed, "the decency . . . intelligence and property of the state [had been] subjected to the domination of its ignorant black pauper multitude."[5] To Pike, black people were children of "vice . . . ignorance and superstition."[6] Their

enslavement and emancipation had not altered this state of affairs;
black people were barbarians unsuited to the task of participat-
ing in government.

> What [the Negro] might have been capable of, under different con-
> ditions that those in which he has ever existed, it is useless to in-
> quire. Races of men exhibit the same general characteristics from
> age to age. The question which concerns us is, not what might be,
> or what in some remote future may be, but what now is. The Negro
> is suddenly thrust into conspicuous prominence in our political
> system, and it is his present condition, qualities, habits, propen-
> sities, that we have to deal with, and we are now all alike deeply in-
> terested with his former masters in considering the problem of his
> character. He is certainly not the kind of man, and his race is not
> the race, for whom our political institutions were originally made;
> and it is already a serious question whether he is the man, or his the
> race, for which they are adapted. We have but barely entered upon
> the experience which is to furnish a solution of this question. It is
> one we need to study and try to master. The overshadowing mass of
> black barbarism at the South hangs like a portentous cloud upon
> the horizon.[7]

Pike was not alone in seeing Negroes as manumitted grotesques
who posed a threat to civilization as white men knew it. A Democratic Kentucky newspaper plumbed the depths of nineteenth-
century white racial fears when it published the following item:

> The graveyards you have selected, beautified, and adorned as a
> resting-place of those you have loved must be desecrated to satisfy
> the spite of those liberty lovers, and choice places given to the
> Negro, even if it should require the exhuming of friends long
> buried. You must divide your pew in church, even if your wife and
> child are forced to sit on the floor, and no complaint must be made
> should Sambo besmear the carpet you have placed there with juice
> of tobacco. Your children at school must sit on the back seats and
> in the cold, whilst the Negro's children sit near the stove and on the
> front seats, and enjoy in every instance the money you toil for,
> whilst Sambo is sleeping and stealing. Or, as the darky explained to
> his less posted brother: "We's gwine to ride free on de railroads,

smoke in de ladies' car, and put our feet on the percushions of the
seats whenever we damn please. We's gwine to be allowed to stop at
de hotels, an set at de head of de table, and hab de biggest slice ob
de chickens, and lay around in de parlors and spit on de carpts,
and make de white trash hustle themselves and wit on us without
grumblin'. We's gwine to be allowed to go to de white schools and
set upon the platform with de teacher. We's gwine to be buried in
italic coffins on top of de white folks, and Gabriel shall call: 'All ob
you colored gemmen rise furst.'[8]

What underlay both Pike's pessimism about the Negroes' abili-
ties and the newspaper's caricature of black freedom was a deeply
held American belief in Negro inferiority. To nineteenth-century
white society, the Civil War had been a Darwinian struggle. A
strong North had defeated a weaker South. Then something unnatural had occurred: a weak and intellectually deficient people,
without history, had been placed in positions of authority over
Anglo-Saxons. In allowing this the North had erred. When historians, both amateurs and professionals, began to evaluate this
period of American history in the 1890s they uniformly condemned the North's actions.

James Ford Rhodes, the author of a seven-volume history of
the United States, used terms like "repressive" and "uncivilized"
to describe Reconstruction.[9] More lurid language was employed
by John W. Burgess, a contemporary of Rhodes, to depict the
Republican plan of Reconstruction. To Burgess the effort to bring
democratic government to the South had been a "hideous tyr-
anny," a "crime against civilization," and a "vile plague."[10] This
line of argument was also advanced in the scholarly work of
William A. Dunning and his students Walter L. Flemming and
Woodrow Wilson.[11] In the popular media, Thomas Dixon in a tril-
ogy of novels — *The Leopard's Spots* (1902), *The Clansmen* (1905),
and *The Traitor* (1907) — "told the 'true story' of the South."[12]
Dixon's fantasies of Reconstruction as racial mongrelization or
rape became, in the hands of the moviemaker D.W. Griffith, "A
Flashing Vision." Griffith's epic film, *Birth of a Nation*, Claude G.
Bowers's popular history, *The Tragic Era*, and Margaret Mitchell's

novel, *Gone with the Wind*, were the cultural icons that popu-
larized the idea that Reconstruction had been an "unnatural act."[13]

It was to refute the myth of Negro incompetence that lay at
the heart of the "Tragic Legend" that W.E. Burghardt DuBois
wrote in 1935 his influential work *Black Reconstruction in America*. "Myth" as I am using it here means more than a false story.
My understanding of myth and how it works as a cultural phenomenon has been greatly influenced by Richard Slotkin's discussion of this problem in *The Fatal Environment*. "Myths are stories,
drawn from history," Slotkin writes, "that have acquired through
usage over many generations a symbolizing function that is central
to the cultural functioning of the society that produces them. . . .
In the end myths become part of the language, as a deeply en-
coded set of metaphors that may contain all of the 'lessons' we
have learned from our history, and all of the essential elements
of our world view."[14] The lesson postbellum America drew from
Reconstruction was that it had been a mistake. The Negro had been
given an opportunity to participate in government and had bungled
it. Even before Reconstruction, the idea of Negro inadequacy had
served a crucial cultural function in America by distinguishing
the free from the unfree. The myth of Reconstruction as disaster
reinforced the idea of Negro inferiority and irresponsibility. Emancipation and Reconstruction had destroyed the South's racial hierarchy. The Negroes had been set free in a world in which they
were unprepared to make their way. This, I take it, was the underlying assumption of the distinguished southern historian Ulrich B.
Phillips when he called the plantation a "school." According to
Phillips the plantation school inculcated in the "commoner" slave
a sense of "routine efficiency, regularity and responsibility."
It also taught "by precept [and] by example . . . furnishing models
of speech and conduct."[15] Inherent in this analysis of black education was an idea that set blacks off from other groups that had
come to America: the belief that any culture or sense of order
that blacks possessed was a product of white tutelage. Even this
idea was qualified. John R. Commons stated that qualification
when he observed that "other races of immigrants, by contact

with our institutions, have been civilized – the Negro has been only domesticated."[16] Without the white man, as Hegel had suggested in his *Philosophy of History,* black people were not capable of "development or culture."[17] To DuBois this idea was anathema.

W.E.B. DuBois was born three years after the conclusion of the Civil War and was educated at Fisk, Harvard, and the University of Berlin. For DuBois, the central fact in his life was race. Speaking on his ninety-first birthday in a speech carried over Peking radio, DuBois remarked, "In my own country for nearly a century I have been nothing but a nigger."[18] This bitter statement reflects the impact of race on DuBois's life. DuBois was a sensitive and highly educated black man, but in American society his accomplishments counted for nothing, he thought. Despite his Harvard Ph.D., W.E.B. DuBois was only "a nigger." But his being a "nigger," I would argue, gave him a particular angle from which to view the history of the American republic. As an outsider looking in, DuBois was able to view the American past from the position of the disadvantaged and excluded. Thus when DuBois came to write *Black Reconstruction*, race occupied a central place in his analysis. For DuBois, race was not a biological datum but something socially constructed. DuBois made this point in his book *Dusk of Dawn* in 1940, and I will have more to say about this later on.[19]

Black Reconstruction, which was published in 1935, is a controversial work. It has been hailed by Marxist scholars as a pioneering piece of social history and viewed by non-Marxists as an important but problematic work of revisionist scholarship.[20] My analysis of the book places me in the latter category. Although DuBois used a Marxist vocabulary and placed emphasis on economics as the engine of social change in America, his monograph is not really a systematic materialist analysis of history. DuBois never really accepted a key tenet of Marxism, that is, the idea of working-class solidarity. What DuBois's personal and intellectual experience told him was that, in America, racial caste and economic class were in conflict. He understood the primacy of race as a "transhistoric" phenomenon in America. Writing of Marxism, he said "this philosophy did not envisage a situation where instead of a horizontal division of classes, there was a vertical fissure, a complete separation of classes by race, cutting square across the economic layers. Even if on one side of this color line, the dark masses were overwhelmingly workers, with but an embryonic capitalist class, nevertheless the split between white and black workers was greater than that between white workers and capitalist; and this split depended not simply on economic exploitation but on a racial folk-lore grounded on centuries of instinct, habit and thought and implemented by the conditional reflex of visible color."[21]

In their attempt to appropriate DuBois as a Marxist, some leftist scholars have ignored the fact that he was at various times in his career ambivalent in his relationship to both the Socialist and Communist parties. This can be seen in an article DuBois published in 1907. He told black people that they did not have to "follow" or "agree" with Socialism "in all things." "I certainly do not," DuBois said. DuBois went on to tell his people that the Socialists were "in trend and ideal . . . the salt of this earth."[22] In 1912 DuBois's ambivalence prevented him from supporting the Socialist candidate for president, Eugene V. Debs. DuBois wrote that he "regarded a vote for Wilson better for Negroes than a vote for Theodore Roosevelt, Taft or an unknown Socialist."[23]

DuBois's major criticism of Socialist thought centered upon the party's handling of the race question. DuBois thought that "the test of any great movement toward social reform [is its treatment of the] excluded class."[24] In America, Negroes constituted this class. The Socialist, afraid of alienating white workers, refused to deal with the "Negro problem." Socialist spokesmen told blacks that "[w]e must not turn aside from the great objects of Socialism to take up this issue of the American Negro; let the question wait; when the objects of Socialism are achieved, the problem will be settled along with other problems."[25] To DuBois, this was arrant nonsense. "The essence of Social Democracy [is] that there shall be no excluded or exploited classes in the Socialistic state, that there shall be no man or woman so poor, ignorant or black as not to count."[26] Although DuBois had faith in Socialism and wanted his people to ally themselves with the Socialists in the ideal of "human brotherhood [and] equality of opportunity,"[27] he had, as I have previously noted, reservations about a dogmatic application of Marxian theory to the United States. "The Marxian philosophy," DuBois observed, "is a true diagnosis of the situation in Europe in the middle of the 19th-century despite some of its logical difficulties. But it must be modified in the United States of America and especially so far as the Negro group is concerned. The Negro is exploited . . . and that exploitation comes . . . from the white capitalist and equally from the white proletariat. . . ."[28] DuBois went on to adumbrate the peculiar position of Negro labor in the United States. He noted that although the "mass of Negroes in the United States [belongs] directly to the working proletariat . . . this black proletariat [is] not a part of the white proletariat."[29]

> . . . while Negro labor in America suffers because of the fundamental inequities of the whole capitalistic system, the lowest and most fatal degree of its suffering comes not from capitalists but from fellow white laborers. It is white labor that deprives the Negro of his right to vote, denies him education, denies him affiliation with trade unions, expels him from decent houses and neighborhoods, and heaps upon him the public insults of open color discrimination.[30]

To DuBois whatever Marx said "concerning the uplift of the working class must, therefore, be modified so far as Negroes are concerned by the fact that he had not studied at first hand their peculiar race problems here in America."[31]

DuBois's criticism of the Marxist analysis of the race problem did not sit well with the Communists. In response to a piece he wrote in 1931 entitled "The Negro and Communism," the Communist Party attacked him savagely. The Communist paper *The Southern Worker* said "the program of the Black Judases has finally been put down in black and white by DuBois. . . ." It was obvious, the paper continued, "that DuBois and other blacks in the NAACP had become 'white man's niggers.'" What DuBois and his cronies had done was "to further split the working class." In this project they were "gratefully supported by the white ruling class."[32] As late as 1936, DuBois could write that "one of the worst things that Negroes could do today, would be to join the American Communist Party." The Communists, DuBois told his readers, "believe, apparently, in immediate violent and bloody revolution, and they are willing to try any and all means of raising hell any-where and under any circumstances. This is a silly program even for white men. For American colored men, it is suicide."[33] If DuBois was not a Marxist in 1935 when he wrote *Black Reconstruction*, then, what was he?

DuBois published his study at a time when the force of Progressive history was still strong in American academic circles. The chief proponents of the Progressive interpretation of American history were Frederick Jackson Turner, Charles A. Beard, and Vernon L. Parrington. These men, as Richard Hofstadter has suggested, wrote a history shaped by the political battles of the Progressive era. Turner, Beard, and Parrington provided the Progressive movement with a useable past and American liberals with a historical tradition. For the Progressive historians ". . . facts" did not "speak for themselves,"[34] but on the contrary, they had no meaning unless they were interpreted and placed in a broader social context. In their work these men also emphasized the moral and social utility of history. History, they believed, taught lessons. The chief lesson to be learned from American history was that the price of liberty was eternal vigilance. Politics was a "conspiratorial process," according to the Progressive historians, and abstractions like equality masked "real" historical forces. As Charles Crowe has written, the Progressive "interpretation of American history . . . stressed economic or geographical forces — or a combination of the two — and found a central theme in the conflict of agrarianism with commercialism and capitalism."[35]

Crowe's description of Progressive history could also be applied to DuBois's *Black Reconstruction*, for the conflict between "economic or geographical forces — or a combination of the two" constitutes a central theme in DuBois's book. What separates

DuBois's study from the work of the Progressive historians, however, is its emphasis on race as a factor in the shaping of American civilization. Charles Beard in his work, for example, never addressed this issue.

To understand *Black Reconstruction* a reader must keep in mind that DuBois was born into a world where race predominated as an ideology. "All is race," declared Disraeli, "there is no other truth."[36] DuBois confirmed Disraeli's observation when he observed in *Dusk of Dawn*:

> Thus in my life the chief fact has been race — not so much scientific race, as that deep conviction of myriads of men that congenital differences among the main masses of human beings absolutely condition the individual destiny of every member of a group. Into the spiritual provincialism of this belief I have been born and this fact has guided, embittered, illuminated and enshrouded my life.[37]

In a world where "color had become an abiding unchangeable fact" DuBois could write: "I felt myself African by 'race' and by that token was African and an integral member of the group of dark Americans who were called Negroes."[38]

What I would like to suggest is that color phobia or racism made DuBois a "race" man. He was never allowed to forget that he was black by the world in which he lived. DuBois, like other black men of his class, was forced to become a defender of the race. In characterizing DuBois as a "race" man I do not want to suggest that he was solipsistic or that he gave up his individuality and became "entombed" in blackness.[39] DuBois defended his people because they had so few articulate champions. He was both a "race" man and a cosmopolite. What DuBois wanted for his people was "the ideal of Race; the ideal of fostering and developing the traits and talents of the Negro, not in opposition to or contempt for other races, but rather in large conformity to the greater ideals of the American Republic, in order that some day on American soil two world-races may give each to each those characteristics both so sadly lack."[40] *Black Reconstruction* was DuBois's effort to demonstrate that this proposition was possible.

DuBois subtitled his book *An Essay toward a History of the Part Which Black Folk Played in the Attempt to Reconstruct Democracy in America, 1860–1880.* In adopting this subtitle DuBois told his readers that he was going to do something that other students of Reconstruction had not done: that is, "to tell and interpret these twenty years of fateful history with especial reference to the efforts and experiences of . . . Negroes themselves."[41] In doing this DuBois placed black people at the center of a crucial period in American history. He made them actors in the nation's past rather than passive, malleable clowns. In doing this, he assaulted what Bernard Weisberger has called "The Dark and Bloody Ground of Reconstruction Historiography."[42] At the heart of the prevailing interpretation of Reconstruction, as I previously noted, was the idea that Negroes were politically incompetent. Professor John W. Burgess, of Columbia University, had expressed this notion savagely in 1902 when he wrote

> The claim that there is nothing in the color of the skin from the point of view of political ethics is a great sophism. A black skin means membership in a race of men which has never of itself succeeded in subjecting passion to reason, has never, therefore, created any civilization of any kind. To put such a race of men in possession of a 'state' government in a system of federal government is to trust them with the development of political and legal civilization upon the most important subjects of human life, and to do this in communities with a large white population is simply to establish barbarism in power over civilization.[43]

To undermine this interpretation, DuBois employed a wide range of primary and secondary historical sources wrapped in Marxist rhetoric.

Black Reconstruction represents the second stage in DuBois's assault on the racist historiography of the Civil War and Reconstruction. In 1910 DuBois had read a paper before the American Historical Association entitled "Reconstruction and Its Benefits."[44] In this paper he argued that Reconstruction had not been a disaster, as white historians claimed.[45] "I was convinced then" DuBois wrote later, "and am more certain since, that the reason for certain adjectives applied to Reconstruction is purely racial. Reconstruction was 'tragic,' 'terrible,' a 'great mistake,' and a 'humiliation,' not because of what actually happened: people suffered after the Civil War, but people suffer after all wars; and the suffering in the South was no greater than in dozens of other centers of murder and destruction. No, the 'tragedy' of Reconstruction was because here an attempt was initiated to make American democracy and the tenets of the Declaration of Independence apply not only to white men, but to black men."[46]

The same thesis was developed in greater depth in *Black Reconstruction*. Reconstruction failed, DuBois argued, because of white cupidity and fear, not because of black incompetence. Calling Reconstruction a "splendid failure," DuBois observed that "it did not fail where it was expected to fail."[47] The book placed great emphasis on economic forces as the engines of social change in America. In doing this, DuBois broke with earlier black historians' emphasis on *ideas* as the motivating force of American historical change.

DuBois's use of Marx was not very successful. His characterization, for example, of both white southern yeomen farmers and the former slaves as "workers" is inaccurate.[48] The white were yeomen farmers and the blacks were ex-slaves whose status at the moment of emancipation was that of landless peasants. Nor at any time did the former slaves ever constitute in a Marxian sense a proletariat.[49] DuBois also erred in describing the drift of slaves away from the plantations to the Union Army as a "General Strike."[50] In leaving the plantations the slaves did not have a political purpose in mind. They were not consciously engaged in some bargaining process with their masters, but were trying to get away from the system that oppressed them. DuBois's observation that during Reconstruction, "in the South, there was being put into force one of the most extraordinary experiments in Marxism that the world, before the Russian Revolution had seen," cannot be taken seriously.[51] In his attempt to make Reconstruction an exercise in class struggle DuBois fails miserably.

Throughout his book, DuBois is forced to confront the fact

that neither southern yeomen nor northern white workers were willing to extend the hand of fellowship to their black peers.

> Thus American labor leaders tried to emphasize the fact that here was a new element, new not in the sense that it had not been there — it had been there all the time — but new in the sense that the Negro worker must now be taken account of, both in his own interest and particularly in their interest. He was a competitor and a prospective under-bidder. Then difficulties appeared, the white worker did not want the Negro in his unions, did not believe in him as a man, dodged the question, and when he appeared at conventions, asked him to organize separately; that is, outside the real labor movement, in spite of the fact that this was a contradiction of all sound labor policy.[52]

What DuBois grapples with here is a problem that all American Marxists have had to deal with: that in America, race has historically taken precedence over class. Thus in the struggle between labor and capital in the United States, white workers, as Aileen Kraditor has written, defined the "class struggle as a sort of private affair among whites — or, to many, white men."[53] As Victor Berger's paper *The Social Democratic Herald* put it on November 30, 1901, "when Marx said: 'Proletarians of all countries unite!' he meant the proletariat of civilized countries, not of Shang-Hay and Timbuctoo."[54]

In chapters 10 and 11 of *Black Reconstruction*, DuBois's application of a class analysis to the freed slaves aspirations is also flawed.[55] The governments established in South Carolina, Mississippi, and Louisiana were better than their predecessors. But DuBois has to confront the fact that the freedmen were capitalist in their sensibilities. What they wanted was land of their own, not socialist cooperatives. As Vernon Lane Wharton noted many years ago: "Their very lives were entwined with the land and its cultivation; they lived in a society where respectability was based on ownership of the soil; and to them to be free was to farm their own ground."[56] Moreover, these people lived in a market economy and many were bourgeois in their aspirations. Writing from the Sea Islands of South Carolina in 1863, a missionary described the industry of a former slave:

He is a black Yankee. Without a drop of white blood in him, he has the energy and 'cuteness' and big eye for his own advantage of a born New Englander. He is not very moral or scrupulous, and the church-members will tell you 'not yet,' with a smile, if you ask whether he belongs to them. But he leads them all in enterprise, and his ambition and consequent prosperity make his example a very useful one on the plantation. Half the men on the island fenced in gardens last autumn, behind their houses, in which they now raise vegetables for themselves and the Hilton Head markets. Limus in his half-acre has quite a little farmyard besides. With poultry-houses, pig-pens, and corn-houses, the array is very imposing. He has even a stable, for he made out some title to a horse, which was allowed; and then he begged a pair of wheels and makes a cart for his work; and not to leave the luxuries behind, he next rigs up a kind of sulky and bows to the white men from his carriage. As he keeps his table in corresponding style, — for he buys more sugar . . . than any other two families, — of course the establishment is rather expensive. So, to provide the means, he has three permanent irons in the fire — his cotton, his Hilton Head express, and his seine. Before the fishing season commenced, a pack of dogs for deer-hunting took the place of the net. While other families 'carry' from three to six or seven acres of cotton, Limus says he must have fourteen. To help his wife and daughters keep this in good order, he went over to the rendezvous for refugees, and imported a family to the plantation, the men of which he hired at $8 a month. . . . With a large boat which he owns, he usually makes weekly trips to the Hilton Head, twenty miles distant, carrying passengers, produce and fish. These last he takes in an immense seine, — an abandoned chattel, — for the use of which he pays Government by furnishing General Hunter and staff with the finer specimens, and then has ten to twenty bushels for sale. Apparently he is either dissatisfied with his arrangement or means to extend his operations, for he asks me to bring him another seine for which I am to pay $70. I presume his savings since 'the guns fired at Bay Point' — which is the native record of the capture of the island — amount to four or five hundred dollars. He is all ready to buy land, and I expect to see him in ten years a tolerably rich man. Limus has, it is true, but few equals on the islands, and yet there are many who follow not far behind him.[57]

I could continue pointing out the failings of *Black Reconstruction* but to do so would be pointless. For when DuBois published his book in 1935, he revolutionized a field of American history.

As I have suggested, prior to the publication of *Black Reconstruction* the historiography of this period was mired in a Manichaean dualism. White was good and black was bad. DuBois showed that this was nonsense. The black regimes of the South, he argued, were the first democratic governments that that section had known. These administrations served both blacks and whites by providing social services which the slavocracy had refused to provide. He also laid to rest the myth that Reconstruction had been a period of fiduciary excess by pointing out that the South's experience during the Grant era was not an exception but the rule. But DuBois did more than this. By focusing on economics, he placed the race question in a broader context, that of the triumph of capital in the nineteenth century over people of color. In so doing he also undermined the idea of American exceptionalism. In DuBois's view, the subordination of the American Negro during Reconstruction was part of a worldwide process whereby whites came to dominate black, brown, and yellow people. Thus, the "race problem" in the United States was not a moral or ethical failure — it was central to the structural evolution of the society and to developments within the world economic system. In emphasizing economics as a fundamental force in shaping American race relations, DuBois broke with his predecessors. Earlier black historians had argued that the "race problem" arose out of a failure of white Americans to implement fully the ideas embodied in the Declaration of Independence and Constitution and that these ideas could be implemented without basic economic change. *Black Reconstruction* was a rejection of this point of view and the presentation of a more critical analysis of the American dilemma.

The American Negro as
Historical Outsider, 1836–1935

The purpose of this essay is to examine the idealist tradition of writing by black historians about the history of blacks in the United States, a tradition which dates back to the second quarter of the nineteenth century and which was ultimately rejected by W.E.B. DuBois in the 1930s. In many ways this history was no different from the American history being written at the same time by many whites. Indeed, it was very Bancroftian in its analysis of the race problem in that it placed great emphasis upon the role of Providence as a force of historical causation. Nevertheless, within the context of the blacks' struggle to find a place in American society the idealist historians' view that history could be an instrument of social change had particular significance. Underlying the work of the black idealists was the belief that history could be used to change the prejudicial attitudes surrounding the Negro, that self-conscious elevation of mind and manners would put prejudice to flight.

The history that blacks wrote in the nineteenth century was a weapon in their people's struggle against an omnipresent "white supremacist" social order. This phrase, borrowed from George Frederickson, aptly describes race relations in both ante- and postbellum America; even after the passage of the Thirteenth, Fourteenth, and Fifteenth Amendments, the United States continued to be a "white supremacist" state, in fact if not in theory. In nineteenth-century America, as Fredrickson writes, there was a "systematic and self-conscious [effort] to make race or color a qualification for membership in the civil community." Further-more, "people of color, however numerous or acculturated they [might] be, [were] treated as permanent aliens or outsiders."[1]

Although they were treated as "aliens or outsiders," the history that black people wrote indicates that they did not think of them-selves as a marginal or peripheral element in American society. They embraced without reservation the ideas embodied in the Constitution and Declaration of Independence. These blacks be-lieved that "all men are created equal, that they are endowed by their Creator with certain unalienable Rights, that among these are Life, Liberty, and the pursuit of Happiness." If blacks had any criticism of America, they deplored its failure to live up to the ideals proclaimed at its eighteenth-century creation. Amer-ica's failings, to them, were moral and ethical, not structural.

The history written in the nineteenth century by Robert Ben-jamin Lewis, William Wells Brown, Martin R. Delany, William Cooper Nell, James Theodore Holly, James W. C. Pennington, Joseph Wilson, and George Washington Williams had a broader purpose than mere popular entertainment. One of its aims was to correct the widely held belief that "the African race is no-toriously idle and improvident" and not characterized by "reason and order." Also, because ignorance of the black past was not confined solely to whites, these writers hoped that their work would be read in the black community. Finally, a history that showed that black people had a glorious past, it was thought, would en-courage American Negroes to acquire "some knowledge of the history of nations" as preparation for the responsibilities of full citizenship.[2] The history that blacks wrote showed that Negroes, regardless of their present status, had in the past been more than hewers of wood and drawers of water.

The first history of black people in America, *Light and Truth*, was written by a man of mixed African and Native American parentage named Robert Benjamin Lewis in 1836. In its organiza-tion, content, and argument this book is a model for understanding the writing of black history up through Carter G. Woodson and exemplified in the work of Brown, Pennington, and Williams. Officially titled *Light and Truth; Collected from the Bible and Ancient and Modern History, Containing the Universal History of the Colored and the Indian Race, from the Creation of the World to the Present Time*, it is paradigmatic for a number of histories that follow the same format.[3] In writing his history Lewis was following a precedent set by Richard Allen and Absalom Jones in their pamphlet *A Narrative of the Proceedings of the Colored People During the Awful Calamity in Philadelphia in the Year 1793; and a Refutation of Some Censures Thrown upon Them in Some Publications* (1794).[4] Jones and Allen were defending "the race" against what they thought were calumnies, and Lewis did the same in *Light and Truth*. He begins by noting that his work was based on materials collected "from sacred and profane history." His book, he says, is an effort to present "correct knowledge of the Colored and Indian people, ancient and modern." "In this country where the former are subjected to degradation — where every variety of persecution is measured out to this unfortunate race," Lewis wrote, "it is highly expedient that 'Light and Truth' should be promulgated, in order that oppressors shall not consider it an indispensable duty to trample upon the week and defenseless" (4). Lewis goes on to observe that the poor race relations in the United States were an aberration and not a general rule worldwide: "In some countries a mighty contrast is visible, colored men enjoy every inherent attainment, free from human interference" (304).

Lewis suggests that many ancient civilizations were Ethiopian and thus Negroid in origin, arriving at this conclusion by tracing the history of humanity after the Creation and Flood. He concludes that black people were the descendants of Ham, the son of Noah. To the descendants of Ham he gives the name "Ethiopian." In denominating blacks as Ethiopians he claims to be following the lead of a Greek historian who is not otherwise identified. He also asserts that a number of oustanding figures of the ancient world were black. Scipio Africanus, Belisarius, Cicero, Hannibal, Moses, Pompey, Terence, and Tertullian were all men of color, according to Lewis (9–30, 192–97, 313–14, and ch. 4).

Lewis's lead was followed by William Wells Brown and James Pennington, who also gave their people a glorious past. Refuting the assertion that blacks had been enslaved because of Noah's curse on Ham, Pennington states that "there is no evidence that Noah's curse was intended to extend to the posterity of Canaan." Black people were descended "from Noah," Pennington says, "through Ham, and from Ham through Cush," and so on. Ultimately Pennington concludes that Negroes were "properly the sons of Cush and Misraim amalgamated." Pennington also contests the idea that because people were called African they were Negroid. The word "Ethiopian," he writes, "is a name derived from the complexion of the inhabitants, while Africa is a name given to a tract of country inhabited by nations of various complexions" (*A Textbook*, 15, 11, 12, 27). Pennington's suggestion that not all Africans were black escaped William Wells Brown, who writes that the "Egyptians . . . were colored and had curled hair." Brown also asserts that the "Ethiopians were an African branch of the Cushites who settled first in Asia" (*Rising Son*, 45–46).

The heavy emphasis that the histories by Brown, Lewis, and Pennington placed upon the exegesis of biblical texts and ancient histories was more than an exercise in antiquarianism. In claiming that their people were the descendants of ancient and noble civilizations that had given the world art, literature, science, and men of great accomplishment,[5] these historians were attempting to establish the unity of humankind. "God is not only the all-glorious author . . . of the black man's mind as well as of that of the white man," according to Pennington, "but he has produced it in the same way identically" (58). The stress that these historians placed upon the unity of humanity contradicted the idea of polygenesis, or the distinct origins of different races, which became popular in some American intellectual circles in the 1840s and 1850s.[6] At the same time, their histories provided a framework within which black people could interpret their people's role in the world's history. This system stood as a counterweight to a history which William Wells Brown described as having "thrown the colored man out."[7]

In giving blacks a role in history, nineteenth-century black historians and spokesmen adopted an interpretive framework that showed how deeply influenced they had been by Christianity and the idea of progress. Howard Dodson has ably summarized this framework as focusing on the following themes: "the great African civilizations of antiquity; outstanding black men and women in American and world history; black achievements in the arts, culture and politics; the contributions of blacks to world civilization; black participation in the major events of American history, particularly its wars; white America's mistreatment of blacks during slavery, reconstruction and the era of segregation."[8] When blacks assessed this concatenation of events, they saw an unfolding of progress.

During the nineteenth century, black and white evangelical Protestants believed that history was progressive and that God was history's prime mover. They also saw themselves as being elect, chosen and covenanted with God to effect his purposes for the world. While blacks and whites shared a common belief system, however, they used the system for different purposes. White Americans used it to conquer a continent and to demonstrate America's providential role in the history of humanity. Their black compatriots discerned a different purpose in God's providential system: to elevate the race in America and Africa.[9] They believed that the Negroes' achievement in the United States was part of a providential plan. God in his mysterious way was using the Negro for beneficial ends, and the blacks' passage from slavery to freedom was the clearest evidence of this progress.[10]

No black spokesperson or intellectual in the nineteenth century thought that God had willed Negroes to be slaves for white Americans, but even slavery and the slave trade could be interpreted as part of a providential design. "God seeing the African standing in need of civilization, sanctioned for a while the slave trade," Henry M. Turner told an Emancipation Day celebration in 1866, "not that it was in harmony with his fundamental laws for one man to rule another, nor did he ever contemplate that the Negro was to be reduced to the status of a vassal, but as a subject for moral and intellectual culture. So God winked, or lidded his eyeballs, at the institution of slavery as a test of the white man's obedience, and elevation of the negro."[11] Despite human cupidity, God's purpose for blacks would be realized. In short, God would bring good out of evil. "Slavery was but a circumstance," according to Bishop L.H. Holsey, "or a link in the transitions of humanity."[12] As Leonard Sweet has suggested, however, these explanations of the why of slavery were abstractions.[13] Blacks still had to face the question of why God permitted the evil of slavery. This too they explained by the theory of its being providential.

The blacks who addressed the question noted that Africa once had had a high degree of civilization. Africa's fall had occurred, according to Pennington, because the Africans had abandoned monotheism and embraced polytheism, "a grand error" (*A Textbook*, 32). Maria Stewart attributed Africa's decline to "gross sins and abominations."[14] George Washington Williams also attributed the Negroes' enslavement to "sin" and "idolatry" (*History*, I: 24). Although these people saw God's hand in the enslavement of blacks, they did not see God's providence as somehow restraining or limiting human will. Indeed, the notion of human beings as historical actors became what Earl Thorpe has called "the central theme of black history."[15] The histories written by Brown, Lewis, Pennington, and Williams depict black people as shapers of their own destiny. In these books and others written during the nineteenth century, blacks are not passive. They resist slavery, become free, acquire property, build institutions, and fight in America's wars.[16] This last activity is particularly noteworthy, because if there was one area of America's history of which black people were particularly proud, it was of their participation in the American Revolution, the War of 1812, and the Civil War.[17]

That they had participated in these struggles, blacks thought, proved that they were the equals of whites. Anyone who reads

Brown's *The Negro in the American Rebellion* or Nell's *The Colored Patriots of the American Revolution* sees this clearly. Both celebrate black accomplishments in war—specifically in the two struggles that determined the future of the American Republic. According to Brown and Nell, the American Revolution and the Civil War enabled black men to show white America that they were manly.[18] In a culture which defined masculinity or manliness in terms of belligerent behavior, black men had shown a willingness to defend their country and to die for it. These and other black historians of their era believed that participation in these struggles and the efforts of blacks to improve themselves entitled black people to citizenship. "Certainly," Martin R. Delany writes in 1852, "there need be no further proof required . . . to show the claims and practical utility of colored people as citizen members of society. We have shown, that in proportion to their numbers, they view and compare favorably in point of means and possessions, with the class of citizens who from chance of superior advantages, have studiously contrived to oppress and deprive them of equal rights and privileges, in common with themselves" (*The Condition*, 109–10).

Delany and the other black historians who wrote in celebration and defense of the Negro used a common methodology: their history was narrative, not analytical. Within these narrative structures, character sketches of people and their careers were the basic units of exposition. One character sketch followed another; none of the sketches was more important than any other. This is not to say that all the depictions were equal in length. Some portraits were longer than others because there was more information about these individuals. When combined, the sketches created a panorama of black achievement. Taking what Thomas Macaulay called the "dross of history," these black historians heaped "particular upon particular,"[19] erecting an intellectual edifice that reflected both a belief in progress and a faith in the power of individuals to effect improvements in their own lives and the condition of their race.

The creation of a black entrepreneurial class in the second half of the nineteenth century did not diminish or alter the animus most American whites felt toward blacks. The accomplishments of a black elite did not stop Caucasians from characterizing Negroes as lazy, spendthrift, irrational, and licentious, in sharp contrast to the perceived white characteristics of intelligence, industriousness, morality, and sexual restraint. In a society undergoing rapid social and economic change, the presence of blacks told whites — in both the North and the South — who they were and were not at a time when they were groping for self-definition. In this context, black efforts at self-improvement were viewed as subversive. Black assertion of any kind provoked a reaction among whites described by Antonio Gramsci as "common sense" ideology, a mode of thought which is "eclectic and unsystematic" because it accumulates contradictory knowledges within itself.[20] The "common sense" ideology of most nineteenth-century whites objectified Negroes in such a way that their accomplishments could be denied or explained away. Although black historians wanted to claim that successful blacks were examples of what the race could achieve if unfettered, to whites these black achievers were anomalies, their accomplishments not emblematic of the Negro race. They were perceived, as William Simmons's catalog of Negro achievement was titled, only as *Men of Mark*.[21] Their success did not redeem the race; it may, in fact, have made the position of the Negro in American society more precarious, especially after emancipation.

When placed in a broader context, the emphasis that nineteenth-century black historians and other representatives of the race placed upon bourgeoisification and acculturation was not unique. If we broaden our perspective and look at another group of the "Lord's despised few," we see that this tactic may not be unusual for outsiders. Although Jewish emancipation began in the eighteenth century, it took off in the nineteenth.[22] Jews in Europe, like blacks in America, were historically a proscribed group. Their emancipation created problems for them and the societies in which they lived. Jacob Katz has described insightfully what happened to the Jews once they left the ghetto:

It is evident that improvement in the status of the Jews from the time they left the ghetto was only a formal achievement. It did not give them social immunity; derogatory statements, aspersions on their character, and insults to their religious beliefs were still permissible. The relationship between the Jewish community and non-Jewish society was still strained by a heavy historical burden and social tension. This strain by itself can suffice to explain the outbreak of hostility, one need not seek an explanation in the general unrest prevailing in society. Despite the fact that they were now a part of the general social framework, having been recognized as citizens of the state — albeit an inferior class — the Jews were still a discernible and separate group and a problem to themselves and their environment.[23]

Likewise, once Negroes left the plantations they were still a "discernible and separate group." Color barred blacks from acceptance in American society.

Ironically, some blacks in the nineteenth century did not see their color as a problem. They thought that hostility directed toward them reflected a distaste for their condition. Frederick Douglass, for example, could write: "Some people will have it that there is a natural, an inherent, and invincible repugnance in the breast of the white race toward dark-colored people; and some very intelligent colored men think that their proscription is owing solely to the color which nature has given them. . . . My experience, both serious and mirthful combats this conclusion" (402). Martin R. Delany, a great critic of American social mores, also denied that color was the cause of black people's oppression (21). Other black spokesmen also attacked the idea that the Negroes' color excluded them from full participation in American society. "Prejudice is a moral phenomenon," according to Sidney, "a wrong exercise of the sentiments and sympathies, a disease of the will."[24] If color was not the cause of black people's exclusion from American civil life, what was? The writers of black history concluded that it was the black people's condition. If blacks transformed themselves, acquired property, educated their children, and showed thereby that they were respectable and responsible, the disabilities they faced would disappear. In saying that these nineteenth-century blacks placed great emphasis upon social rehabilitation, I do not mean to suggest that they abandoned either protest or agitation as weapons in their quest for equal rights. At the same time, however, it should be noted that they also placed great emphasis upon embourgeoisment as the answer to their problems. In this sense they were similar to certain sectors of nineteenth-century Jewry who also thought that becoming like the "other" would resolve their problems. As Steven Aschheim, Michael Marrus, and William O. McCagg, Jr., have suggested, this process was fraught with difficulties.[25]

German Jews, like blacks, had faith in the "rationality" of the societies in which they lived. In the process of improving themselves, they abandoned those cultural traits that had marked them as outsiders (Aschheim, 7–9, 15, 225) and expected, consequently, to be absorbed into the society. French and some Hungarian Jews followed a similar path (Marrus, 87; McCagg, 18). Unfortunately, both Jews and blacks were thought of as distinct racial types by the people with whom they lived. In transforming themselves — that is, in the case of blacks acculturating, in the case of Jews assimilating — they unsettled the dominant groups in these countries. An 1855 article in the *Allgemeine Zeitung des Judentums* parodied an anti-Semite's anxieties about Jewish assimilation: "The more the old Jew with his sometimes ridiculous aspects fades away, the more Jew hatred increases. One disdained the Jew who made one laugh, but one tolerated and often even liked him; but one hates the Jew in equal position and with equal rights" (cited by Aschheim, 78). Fourteen years later a southern U.S. newspaper ran a piece that bemoaned Negro emancipation: "Aside from this selfish view, slavery was a God-send for the negro race. Negroes as bondsmen, were happier, more sleek, and greasy looking, and better clothed, than they are now. We never hear the ringing horse-laughs, the picking of banjoes, beating of tambourines, and knocking of feet against puncheon floors, that formerly marked their sans souci existence. Instead thereof, they may be heard to grumble, in squads, collected in fence corners, and may be seen with ashey faces, grim countenances and squalid appearances generally."²⁶ These quotations reflect a nostalgia for unassimilated Jews and enslaved blacks. Emancipation liberated the black and Jew from their historic places in society and this, coupled with the other traumas of modernization, fueled the flames of late-nineteenth-century racism and anti-Semitism.

Because the history written by blacks was conceptualized in idealist terms it could not deal with the enduring nature of American racism. Even after the Civil War and Reconstruction, black historians would continue to write optimistically about their people's role and future in the evolution of American society. This can be most clearly seen in George Washington Williams's monumental two-volume *History of the Negro Race in America 1619–1880*. Williams was born in 1849 of racially mixed parentage and was variously a Union soldier, Baptist minister, and Ohio state legislator.²⁷ His book has been celebrated as representing a new departure in Negro historical studies, chiefly because of his claim that in preparing his work he "consulted over twelve thousand volumes"—about one thousand of which are referred to in the footnotes—and "thousands of pamphlets" (1: vi). In terms of its conceptualization and methodology, however, Williams's history represents no break with the tradition begun by Robert Benjamin Lewis.

The history is divided into two parts. The first half is devoted to the Negro's African origins, slavery in the colonies, and the Negro during the Revolution. The second volume, which focuses on the nineteenth century, treats such topics as the antislavery movement, Negro participation in the Civil War, and Reconstruction. There are also chapters on social and cultural history. Williams wrote his history, he says, because he

became convinced that a history of the colored people in America was required, because of the ample historically trustworthy material at hand; because the colored people themselves had been the most vexatious problem in North America, from the time of its discovery down to the present day; because that in every attempt upon the life of the nation, whether by foes from without or within, the colored

people had always displayed a matchless patriotism and an incom-
parable heroism in the cause of Americans, and because such a
history would give the world more correct ideas of colored people,
and incite the latter to greater effort in the struggle of citizenship
and manhood. (1: iii–iv)

Denying that he was a "panegyrist," "Partisan" or "apologist,"
Williams claimed that he wrote "from a love for the truth of
history." In writing the "truth he did not want to revive sectional
animosities or race prejudice." *The History of the Negro Race in
America*—like the earlier work of Brown, Lewis, and Wells—is
extremely moralistic and judgmental in tone. Noting that there
were still racist writers in America, Williams observed that this
is "a sad commentary on American civilization." It does not seem
to have occurred to him that racism was a defining characteristic
of American society. Imbued with a sense of Christian progress,
Williams retreated into the comforting but implausible observation that racist literature in American "no longer has an audience
or readers, not even in the south" (1:108).

Williams was a nineteenth-century black Christian, and when
he looked at the history of the Negro people in America from the
seventeenth to the nineteenth centuries he saw an unfolding of
Christian progress. "To the candid student of ethnography," Williams wrote, "it must be conclusive that the Negro is but the most
degraded and disfigured type of the primeval African." The Negro's
degradation was the result of "sin," "idolatry" and the "invincible
forces of nature" (1: 48, 24, 47). Williams's negative assessment
of Africa reflected the nineteenth-century black belief that Africa
would take its place among the modern nations of the world once
it was Christianized.[28] Having come to America and entered the
Christian fold, blacks became shapers of their own history. They
resisted slavery and became poets, scientists, soldiers, and men of
property. Within this panorama of achievement Williams detected
only one failing, and that had occurred during Reconstruction.
Williams's analysis of the failure of Reconstruction could have
been written by Booker T. Washington:

The government gave [the Negro] the statute-book when he ought
to have had the spelling-book; placed him in the legislature when he
ought to have been in the school-house. In the great revolution that
followed the war, the heels were put where the brains ought to have
been. An ignorant majority, without competent leaders, could not
rule an intelligent Caucasian minority. Ignorance, vice, poverty, and
superstition could not rule intelligence, experience, wealth, and
organization. . . . The Negro governments were built on the shifting
sands of the opinions of the men who reconstructed the south, and
when the storm and rains of political contest came they fell because
they were not built upon the granite foundation of intelligence and
statesmanship.

Then, in a passage which was Darwinian in inspiration, Williams goes
on to say that "it was an immutable and inexorable law which de-
manded the destruction of those governments. It was a law that knows
no country, no nationality. Spain, Mexico, France, Turkey, Russia, and
Egypt have felt its cruel touch to a greater or lesser degree. But a lesson
was taught the colored people that is invaluable. Let them rejoice that
they are out of politics. Let white men rule" (2: 527).

Williams's observations about Reconstruction, written before
Booker T. Washington became a national figure, reflect the general
feeling among some post-Reconstruction blacks that politics were
dangerous and should be left to the white man. Given this reality,
they believed, black people should husband their resources and
develop the black community.[29] Williams concludes his history
on an optimistic note reflecting this sensibility: "Race prejudice
is bound to give way before the potent influence of character, education, and wealth. And these are necessary to the growth of the
race. Without wealth there can be no leisure, without leisure there
can be no thought, and without thought there can be no progress" (2: 551–52). Williams's hopefulness was shared by the senior
class at Tuskegee Insitute which in 1886 adopted as its class motto
the statement, "There Is Room at the Top."[30] These cheerful comments about the Negro's future in America have to be measured
against the harsh reality that blacks confronted in the last quarter
of the nineteenth century: violence and the rise of scientific racism.

Between 1885 and 1894 seventeen hundred Negroes were lynched in America.[31] Most of this violence took place in the South, but it reflected a national mood in which the Negro was objectified as subhuman. Late-nineteenth-century American racists possessed something their antebellum predecessors lacked, a science or pseudoscience of race. Developed in Europe in the late nineteenth century, these ideas became popular in America in the 1880s.[32] Borrowing Darwin's idea of survival of the fittest, "race scientists," as John Higham has written, "subsumed mankind under the grim physical laws of the animal kingdom."[33] In the struggle for survival the Negro was a major loser. He had been captured, enslaved, and brought to America by the superior Anglo-Saxon, and whatever progress the Negro made in the New World was attributable to his white teachers. This mode of thought deeply influenced the writing of American history in the 1880s. Following the lead of German scholarship, American historians focused on the comparative study of developing institutions and employed biological metaphors and analogies to explain the evolution of society. Herbert Baxter Adams, for example, taught his students that democratic institutions had originated in the forests of Central Europe and from there had been carried by Germanic peoples to England and North America.[34] Negroes were classed with the Irish and what John Burgess called "the rabble from southern and southeastern Europe."[35] They were outsiders, aliens. Although blacks had been present in North America since 1619, they were not Americans in the same way that Anglo-Saxons were. They lacked both a history of self-government and cultural achievement. Moreover, when given a chance to share in Reconstruction governments, blacks had failed. In contrast to the wider context in which it was placed by George Washington Williams, this perceived failure was interpreted by white historians as proof of the Negro's innate inferiority. Thus, for example, Woodrow Wilson wrote of Reconstruction: "Here was a vast 'laboring, landless, homeless class,' once slaves, now free; unpracticed in liberty, unschooled in self-control; never sobered by the discipline of self-support, never established in any habit of prudence; excited by a freedom they did not understand, exalted by false hopes, bewildered and without leaders, and yet insolvent and aggressive; sick of work, covetous of pleasure—a host of dusky children untimely put out of school."[36] Other immigrants to America had been "civilized," John R. Commons observed; the Negro had only been "domesticated."[37]

These comments about Negro character indicate how negligible an impact the history written by Lewis and his successors had had upon American racial thought before 1915.[38] The history written by whites was supposedly based on a complete evaluation of the evidence available to scholars; but a "common sense" ideology buttressed by a science of race made it impossible for the Negro to be treated as a responsible citizen in history books written by white scholars. This can be seen most clearly in the literature proceeding out of the Civil War and Reconstruction.[39] Several scholars have noted that this scholarship was pro-southern and racist,[40] but in addition it created a crisis for blacks writing history in America. This was particularly true for the first two Negroes to receive Ph.D.'s in history, W.E.B. DuBois and Carter G. Woodson.

Both DuBois and Woodson were products of that black Victorian culture which flourished in America after Emancipation. They both initially thought that condition—not color—was the great barrier to Negro progress. Writing about his early life, DuBois reminisced that his mother had taught him that "the secret of life and the loosening of the color bar . . . lay in excellence, in accomplishment . . . there was no real discrimination on account of color—it was all a matter of ability and hard work."[41] Both DuBois and Woodson were to find out that hard work alone would not redeem the Negro, but this realization led the two historians to differing methodologies and conclusions. While Woodson's work remained within the tradition established by Lewis, DuBois broke new ground by placing the history of the Negro in a broader conceptual framework.

Carter G. Woodson was born in 1875 in New Canton, Virginia. His parents were former slaves turned sharecroppers. Between 1897 and 1901 he attended Berea College in Kentucky, and after receiving a teaching certificate he taught high school in West Virginia. He also took correspondence courses from the University of Chicago. After working in the Philippines and traveling in Europe and Africa, he enrolled as a full-time student at the University of Chicago in 1907. A year later he enrolled at Harvard to study for the Ph.D., and he received that degree in 1912.[42]

Woodson's entry into the historical profession occurred at a significant moment in the history of the Negro people in America, that of the nationalization of the race problem. Prior to 1914 the majority of black people had lived in the South, but during World War I a large number of blacks migrated north in search of better economic and social opportunities. They were to be disappointed. In the North they found the racism which had haunted their lives to be alive and well. It was in this context that Woodson founded the Association for the Study of Negro Life and Culture in 1915 and began publishing *The Journal of Negro History*. The Association, as it came to be called, was not the first organization devoted to the study of black history.[43] What distinguished Woodson's endeavor from those of his predecessors was his single-mindedness. He was the Association's director from 1915 to 1950, and under his leadership it flourished.

Woodson was a mediocre historian whose books were written in a rather pedestrian style.[44] His great talent lay in the acquisition of historical materials pertaining to the Negro, documents which for the most part white historians had either ignored or dismissed as worthless.[45] In uncovering these materials Woodson saw himself as correcting the bias of white historians. According to him, white historians made "little effort to set forth what the race has thought and felt and done as a contribution to the world's accumulation of knowledge and the welfare of mankind." The Negro was "a negligible factor in the thought of most historians, except to be mentioned only to be condemned."[46]

In uncovering the Negro's past, Woodson wanted to instill pride in his people and show whites that blacks had a history too. According to Woodson, "one race has not accomplished any more good than any other race, for God could not be just and at the same time make one race the inferior of the other. But if you leave it to the one to set forth his own virtues while disparaging those of others, it will not require many generations before all credit for human achievements will be ascribed to one particular stock. Such is the history taught the youth today." "On the other hand," he continues, "just as thorough education in the belief in the inequality of races has brought the world to the cat-and-dog stage of religious and racial strife, so may thorough instruction in the equality of races bring about a reign of brotherhood through an appreciation of the virtues of all races, creeds and colors." He then concludes with the following exhortation:

> Let the light of history enable us to see that "enough of good there is in the lowest estate to sweeten life; enough of evil in the highest to check presumption; enough there is of both in all estates to bind us in compassionate brotherhood, to teach us impressively that we are of one dying and immortal family." Let truth destroy the dividing prejudices of nationality and teach universal love without distinction of race, merit or rank. With the sublime enthusiasm and heavenly vision of the Great Teacher let us help men to rise above the race hate of this age unto the altruism of a rejuvenated universe.

For Woodson believed that "prejudice . . . is not something inherent in human nature,"[47] but that it is something that is learned. In arguing this he may have had in mind a political purpose: he may have been seeking some sort of *rapprochement* with whites. He noted in an essay published in 1919 that an "enlightened class" of southern whites was taking an interest in black history: "Seeing that a better understanding of the races is now necessary to maintain that conservatism to prevent this country from being torn asunder by Socialism and Bolshevism, they are now making an effort to effect a closer relation between . . . blacks and whites by making an intensive study of the Negro."[48] The possibility that this scrutiny may have been motivated by reactionary intentions escaped Woodson. Although he was significant as a professionally trained scholar who attempted to place the history of the American Negro in a comparative framework, Woodson's work was conceptually weak.[49]

Like a number of his predecessors, Woodson continued to conceptualize the race problem as a moral failing on the part of black and white Americans. His peer W.E.B. DuBois was the first black scholar to break out of this mold. When DuBois published his *Black Reconstruction*, Negro history was in a state of crisis rooted in the inability of black historical scholarship to explain the continuing oppression of Negroes in America. Despite having acquired property, become educated, and fought in American wars, Negroes were still second-class citizens. Their efforts to join the American mainstream were still rebuffed. DuBois found the explanation of this state of affairs through the application of a mixture of racial romanticism and Marxism.

W.E.B. DuBois was born in 1868 and was educated at Fisk and Harvard and the University of Berlin.[50] He was probably the most knowledgeable American empirical historical sociologist of his time. DuBois's great erudition was put to the task of ending the race problem, but before he could undertake this he had to escape the constraints imposed by a late-nineteenth-century university education. Commenting on his education later in life, DuBois said: "We studied history and politics almost exclusively from the point of view of ancient German freedom, English and New England democracy, and the development of the United States." Where did black people fit into this schema? At Harvard, wrote DuBois, "it was continually stressed in the community and in the classes that there was a vast difference in the development of the whites and the 'lower' races; that this could be seen in the physical development of the Negro."[51]

To overcome this mountain of prejudice DuBois embarked on a scientific study of the race problem,[52] believing that "science" and "truth" would triumph over "a mass of self-conscious instincts and unconscious prejudices."[53] Although he was trained in the scientific method, DuBois was also a racial romantic, and his work shows a fusion of these two strains of thought. His racial romanticism can be most clearly seen in his essay "The Conservation of the Races" (1897) and in his *Souls of Black Folk* (1903).[54]

In "The Conservation of the Races" DuBois described his race with considerable hyperbole: "We are Americans, not only by birth and by citizenship, but our political ideals, our language, our religion. Farther than that, our Americanism does not go. . . . We are . . . the harbinger of that to-morrow which is yet destined to soften the whiteness of the Teutonic today. We are that people whose subtle sense of song has given America its only American music, its only American fairy tales . . . its only touch of pathos and humor amid its mad money-getting plutocracy" (11–12). In reading this passage one is led to assume that somehow blacks had after 278 years in this country shielded themselves from the grossest material excesses of American culture. The same romantic sensibility infuses the oft-quoted passage about black people possessing a double consciousness. Was DuBois talking about the Negro people or himself when he wrote in *The Souls of Black Folk* of an "American, a Negro; two souls, two thoughts, two unreconciled strivings, two warring ideals in one dark body"? (16–17). DuBois's work, I would like to suggest, moved from this romantic racialism to a more insightful analysis of the race problem in *Black Reconstruction*.

What caused this transformation in DuBois's thinking was the failure of scientific study to undermine racism: "I had come to the place where I was convinced that science, the careful social study of the Negro problems, was not sufficient to settle them; that they were not basically, as I had assumed, difficulties due to ignorance but rather difficulties due to the determination of certain people to suppress and mistreat the darker races." A page farther in *Dusk of Dawn* he tells us that he arrived at this conclusion in the wake of World War I: "Little did I realize in August, 1910, the earth was about to be shaken with earthquake, deluged with blood, whipped and starved into disaster, and that race hate and wholesale color and group subordination, not only was a prime cause of this disaster, but emphasized and sharpened its course and hindered consequent recovery" (221–22). His awakening to the pervasiveness of racism also meant, as Allison Davis has argued, that DuBois rejected "the Black middle-class belief that education would overcome white prejudice and oppression."[55] These new insights enabled DuBois to end the confusion between culture and politics which had characterized his predecessors' works and which was the essential failing of his antagonist Booker T. Washington.

Black Reconstruction represents the second stage in DuBois's assault on the racist historiography of the Civil War and Reconstruction. In 1910 he had read a paper before the American Historical Association entitled "Reconstruction and Its Benefits."[56] This paper argued that Reconstruction had not been a disaster, as white historians claimed.[57] As DuBois wrote in *Dusk of Dawn*: "I was convinced then, and am more certain since, that the reason for certain adjectives applied to Reconstruction is purely racial. Reconstruction was 'tragic,' 'terrible,' a 'great mistake,' and a 'humiliation,' not because of what actually happened: people suffered after the Civil War, but people suffer after all wars; and the suffering in the South was no greater than in dozens of other centers of murder and destruction. No, the 'tragedy' of Reconstruction was because here an attempt was initiated to make American democracy and the tenets of the Declaration of Independence apply not only to white men, but to black men" (318–19).

The same thesis was developed in greater depth twenty-five years later in *Black Reconstruction*, where DuBois argued that Reconstruction failed not because of black incompetence but because of white cupidity and fear. Calling Reconstruction a "splendid failure," DuBois observes that "it did not fail where it was expected to fail."[58] The book places great emphasis on economic forces as the engines of social change in America. In doing this DuBois broke with earlier black historians' emphasis on ideas as the motivating force of American historical change. By focusing on economics, he placed the race question in a broader context, that of the triumph of capital over people of color in the nineteenth century. In so doing he also undermined the idea of American exceptionalism. In DuBois's view, the subordination of the American Negro during Reconstruction was part of a worldwide process whereby whites came to dominate black, brown, and yellow people. Thus, the race problem in the United States was not a moral or ethical failure—it was central to the structural evolution of the society and to developments within the world economic system.

DuBois's embracing of Marx came late in his career and was not complete.[59] Unlike some young black scholars, DuBois did not employ a vulgar class analysis in his study of Reconstruction.[60] He understood the primacy of race as a "transhistoric" phenomenon in America. Writing of Marxism, he points out that "this philosophy did not envisage a situation where instead of a horizontal division of classes, there was a vertical fissure, a complete separation of classes by race, cutting square across the economic layers. Even if on one side of this color line, the dark masses were overwhelmingly workers, with but an embryonic capitalist class, nevertheless the split between white and black workers was greater than that between white workers and capitalists; and this split depended not simply on economic exploitation but on a racial folk-lore grounded on centuries of instinct, habit and thought and implemented by the conditional reflex of visible color" (*Dusk of Dawn*, 205).

DuBois's employment of a quasi-Marxist analysis was hailed by one black scholar as a great breakthrough in the study of American black history.[61] Certainly *Black Reconstruction* is more than just a revisionist piece of historical scholarship. It constitutes an important turning point in the evolution of American Negro historiography, representing a break with a form of historical writing which was largely idealist in its conceptualization, and initiating a move toward a materialist analysis of black history. Most black scholars did not follow DuBois's lead. The history written, for example, by John Hope Franklin and Benjamin Quarles would continue to reflect an idealist analysis of the race problem, in the tradition of Robert Benjamin Lewis and his nineteenth-century successors. Why these historians did not follow DuBois's lead constitutes an important chapter in American black intellectual history whose treatment is, however, beyond the range of this essay.

Notes

Introduction

1. John W. Blassingame, *The Slave Community* (New York, 1972); Herbert G. Gutman, *The Black Family in Slavery and Freedom, 1750–1925* (New York, 1976); Vincent Harding, *There Is a River* (New York, 1981); George Rawick, *From Sundown to Sunup* (Westport, Conn., 1972); Sterling Stuckey, *Slave Culture* (new York, 1987); Thomas L. Webber, *Deep Like the Rivers* (New York, 1978). I have not included Lawrence W. Levine's *Black Culture and Black Consciousness* (New York, 1977) in this group of books. Levine's argument about black culture pays close attention to the master's power in the master-slave relationship (see 73 and 99). Charles Joyner's *Down by the Riverside* (Urbana, Ill., 1984) also takes into account the role of the master's power both in the fields and cabins (see 41). The genesis of what I call the slave community/culturalist paradigm is discussed in August Meier and Elliott Rudwick, *Black History and the Historical Profession, 1915–1980* (Urbana, Ill., 1986), ch. 4.

2. Nick Salvatore, "Two Tales of a City: Nineteenth Century Black Philadelphia," *Dissent,* (Spring, 1991), 227–235.

3. W.E.B. DuBois, *The Philadelphia Negro: A Social Study* (1899; New York, 1967); E. Franklin Frazier, *The Negro Family in the United States* (Chicago, 1939); Kenneth B. Clark, *Dark Ghetto: Dilemmas of Social Power* (New York, 1965); Daniel Patrick Moynihan, "The Negro Family: The Case for National Action," in Lee Rainwater and William L. Yancy, eds., *The Moynihan Report and the Politics of Controversy* (Cambridge, Mass., 1967); Abram Kardiner and Lionel Ovesey, *The Mark of Oppression* (Cleveland, 1962).

4. For an interesting analysis of the emergence of black history as a field of study see Meier and Rudwick, *Black History and the Historical Profession.* See also Darlene Clark Hine, ed., *The State of Afro-American History: Past, Present, and Future* (Baton Rouge, 1986).

5. For criticisms of this change see Diane Ravitch, *America Revised* (Boston, 1979), and Thomas Bender, "Wholes and Parts: The Need for Synthesis in American History," *The Journal of American History* 73 (1986), 120–36.

6. See, for example, Levine, *Black Culture and Black Consciousness,* chs. 1 and 2 passim.

7. Blassingame, *The Slave Community,* 105. Blassingame contradicts his observation about the slave community in 105: "In the final analysis, the character of the antebellum plantation was one of the major determinants of the attitudes, perceptions and behavior of the slave."

8. Rawick, *From Sundown to Sunup,* introduction, xix.

9. Webber, *Deep Like the Rivers,* 262.

10. Kenneth M. Stampp, *The Peculiar Institution* (New York, 1956).

11. Bertram Wyatt-Brown, "The Mask of Obedience: Male Slave Psychology in the Old South," *The American Historical Review* 93 (1988), 1230; see also the excellent articles by Peter Kolchin, "Reevaluating the Antebellum Slave Community: A Comparative Perspective," *The Journal of American History* 70 (1983), 579–601; "American Historians and Antebellum Southern Slavery, 1959–1984," in William J. Cooper, Michael F. Holt, and John McCardell, eds., *A Master's Due: Essays in Honor of David Herbert Donald* (Baton Rouge, 1985), 86–111; and Laurence Shore, "The Poverty of Tragedy in Historical Writing on Southern Slavery," *The South Atlantic Quarterly* 85 (1986), 147–64. These articles raise important questions about the slave community/culturalist paradigm. See also the splendid analysis of slavery in Orlando Patterson, "Toward a Study of Black America: Notes on the Culture of Racism," in *Dissent* (Fall 1989), 476–86.

12. The quoted phrase is from Laurence Shore, "Poverty of Tragedy," 148.

13. Gutman, *Black Family,* 33. For a thoughtful critique of this tendency in Gutman's work see Mike Kazin, "The Historian as Populist," *The New York Review of Books,* May 12, 1988, p. 48.

14. Ibid., 32.

15. W.E.B. DuBois, *The Souls of Black Folk,* in John Hope Franklin, ed., *Three Negro Classics* (1903; New York, 1965), 346.

16. Quoted in Wyatt-Brown, "The Mask of Obedience," 1236. For another example of a slave overawed by his master's power see *Father Henson's Story of His Own Life* (1849; New York, 1962), 48–53.

17. Benjamin Drew, *The Refugee: A North-Side View of Slavery* (1855; Reading, Mass., 1969), 105.

18. Quoted in Peter Walker, *Moral Choices* (Baton Rouge, 1978), 241.

19. *Narrative of William Wells Brown*, in Gilbert Osofsky, ed., *Puttin' on Ole Massa* (1874; New York, 1969), 219–20.

20. The essays cited in n. 11 do this.

21. Ellen McEwen, "The Ties that Divide," in V. Burgmann and J. Lee, eds., *Australia since the Invasion: A People's History*, vol. 4 (Sydney, 1988), 27. For an insightful comment on the limitations of an analysis emphasizing community see John E. Toews, "Perspectives on 'The Old History and the New:' A Comment," *The American Historical Review* 94 (1989), 697. Finally, students of slave culture/community paradigm will benefit from reading David Warren Sabean, *Power in the Blood* (Cambridge, Eng., 1987). This book contains some valuable insights about the limits of community as an analytical focus.

22. Laura M. Towne, *Letters and Diaries*, Rupert Sargeant Holland, ed. (1912; New York, 1969), 232.

23. Henry L. Swint, ed., *Dear Ones at Home* (Nashville, 1966), 189. Sterling Stuckey's *Slave Culture* (New York, 1987) contains an interesting discussion of the use of the word "nigger" among slaves, 98.

24. *Colored American*, January 13, 1866. See also the role color prejudice played in the family life of Sara Lawrence Lightfoot, *Balm in Gilead* (New York, 1988), passim.

25. Quoted in James M. McPherson, *Ordeal by Fire* (New York, 1982), 560.

26. Ibid.

27. For an illuminating discussion of community formed in response to oppression see Hannah Arendt, *The Jew As Pariah* (New York, 1978). This book does an excellent job of analyzing the various responses of Jews to anti-Semitism.

28. Gutman, *Black Family*, 61–66. See also Gutman's essay "The Black Family in Slavery and Freedom: A Revised Perspective," in Ira Berlin, ed., *Power and Culture: Essays on the American Working Class* (New York, 1987), 357–79; and "Marital and Sexual Norms among Slave Women," in Nancy F. Cott and Elizabeth H. Pleck, eds., *A Heritage of Her Own* (New York, 1979), 298–310.

29. Harriet A. Jacobs, *Incidents in the Life of a Slave Girl*, Jean F. Yellin, ed. (Cambridge, Mass., 1987), 55–56.

30. "Narrative of Sara Fitzpatrick," in John W. Blassingame, ed., *Slave Testimony* (Baton Rouge, 1977), 646. One slave woman reported that she did not like marriage. See the narrative of Rose Williams in *Bullwhip Days: The Slaves Remember an Oral History*, James Mellon, ed. (New York, 1988), 132. For examples of female slave victimization, see *We Are Your Sisters: Black Women in the Nineteenth Century*, Dorothy Sterling, ed. (New York, 1984), 25–27. "Afro-American Families in the Transition from Slavery to Freedom," in *Radical History Review* 42 (September 1988), Ira Berlin, Steven Miller, and Leslie S. Rowland, eds., contains an interesting document on spouse abuse. (See 99–100.)

31. I am thinking here of the work of Alice Childress, *A Short Walk* (New York, 1979); Toni Morrison, *Beloved* (New York, 1987); Alice Walker, *The Color Purple* (New York, 1982); Sherley Anne Williams, *Dessa Rose* (New York, 1986). For an insightful discussion of the problems facing black women writers, see Calvin C. Hernton, *The Sexual Mountain and Black Women Writers* (New York, 1987). See also Elizabeth Fox-Genovese, *Within the Plantation Household* (Chapel Hill, N.C., 1988). This provocative book contains a number of important statements that correct Herbert Gutman's romanticism about slave family; see, for example, 48–50.

32. Wyatt-Brown, "The Mask of Obedience: Male Slave Psychology in the Old South," 1246.

33. Two recent works that exemplify this tendency are Vincent Harding's *There Is a River* and Sterling Stuckey's *Slave Culture*. See my reviews of these two books. I examine some of the problems of *There Is a River* in "Black Bancroft," *Journal of Ethnic Studies* 11 (1983), 112–18; and *Slave Culture* is critiqued in "Three Books on Race," *Journal of American Ethnic History* 9 (Spring 1990). See also Peter Novick, *That Noble Dream* (New York, 1988). This book contains an insightful critique of black history in ch. 14.

34. See the letters in *The Journal of American History* 75 (1988), 324–27, 328–29. Se also Professor Franklin's letter to the editor of *The Philadelphia Inquirer*, April 15, 1987.

35. Nell Painter, "Who Decides What Is History," *The Nation*, March 6, 1982, p. 277. See also Professor Painter's rhapsodic assessment of Herbert Gutman's career in *Labor History* 29 (1988), 336–54.

36. Quoted in Benjamin Quarles, *Black Abolitionist* (New York, 1969), 56.

37. Jackson Lears, "The Concept of Cultural Hegemony: Problems and Possibilities," *American Historical Review* 90 (June 1985), 373. See also Wilson J. Moses, "Civil Religion, Civil Activism, and Afro-American Identity: Antebellum Black Leaders and the Art of Biography," *Reviews in American History* 18 (March 1990), 55–63. This article is a good place to begin an examination of black history as a problem in the new social history.

38. Charles Beard, *An Economic Interpretation of the Constitution of the United States* (New York, 1935). Beard's work is criticized in Robert E. Brown, *Charles Beard and the Constitution: A Critical Analysis of an Economic Interpretation of the Constitution of the United States* (Princeton, N.J., 1956); and Forrest McDonald, *We the People: The Economic Origins of the Constitution* (Chicago, 1958).

39. Herbert Gutman, *Work, Culture, and Society in Industrializing America: Essays in American Working Class and Social History* (New York, 1976); David Montgomery, *Beyond Equality* (New York, 1967); C. Vann Woodward, *The Origins of the New South* (Baton Rouge, 1951).

40. E.P. Thompson, *The Making of the English Working Class* (London, 1963). The impact of this book on American historians is discussed by Ira Berlin, "Introduction: Herbert G. Gutman and the American Working Class," in Berlin, *Power and Culture*, 3–69; and Alan Dawley, "E.P. Thompson and the Peculiarities of the Americans," *Radical History Review* 19 (1978–79), 33–59.

41. Gareth Stedman Jones, *Languages of Class* (Cambridge, Eng., 1985), 42. Two recent books that reflect a Thompsonian influence are Steven Hahn, *The Roots of Southern Populism* (New York, 1983); and Sean Wilentz, *Chants Democratic: New York City and the Rise of the American Working Class, 1790–1865* (New York, 1984).

42. Mike Kazin's article "A People Not a Class: Rethinking the Political Language of the Modern U.S. Labor Movement," in Mike Davis and Michael Sprinker, eds., *Reshaping the U.S. Left* (New York, 1988), 257–86, is an impressive discussion of this problem.

43. Eric Hobsbawm, *Workers: Worlds of Labor* (New York, 1984), 190.

44. Paul E. Johnson, *A Shopkeeper's Millenium* (New Haven, Conn., 1978).

45. Richard Drinnon, *Facing West* (London, 1980), introduction, xvii.

46. See, for example, Amy Bridges, "Becoming American, The Working Class in the United States before the Civil War," in Ira Katznelson

and Aristide R. Zolberg, eds., *Working-Class Formation* (Princeton, N.J., 1986), 157–96; Barbara J. Fields, "Ideology and Race in American History," in J. Morgan Kousser and James M. McPherson, eds., *Region, Race, and Reconstruction* (New York, 1982); Hahn, *Roots of Southern Populism*, 90; Wilentz, *Chants Democratic*, 264–65, passim. For some work in this field that pays close attention to race see Alexander Saxton, *The Indispensable Enemy: Labor and the Anti-Chinese Movement in California* (Berkeley, Calif., 1971); Gwendolyn Mink, *Old Labor and New Immigrants in American Political Development* (Ithaca, 1986); Richard Slotkin, *The Fatal Environment: The Myth of the Frontier in the Age of Industrialization* (New York, 1985). The new social history in its emphasis on class analysis has also been derelict on the question of gender. See Heidi Hartman, "The Unhappy Marriage of Marxism and Feminism: Towards a More Progressive Union," in Lydia Sargent, ed., *Women and Revolution* (Boston, 1981), 1–41; and Joan Wallach Scott, "Gender: A Useful Category of Historical Analysis," in *Gender and the Politics of History* (New York, 1988), 30. Finally, before this book went to press I read Professor Fields's recent essay "Slavery, Race and Ideology in the United States of America." This essay is an elaboration of ideas adumbrated in "Ideology and Race in American History," which appeared in 1982. Parts of the new essay are more confusing than the 1982 article, and nothing in this recent piece changes my argument in chapter 1. The Fields essay, "Slavery, Race and Ideology in the United States of America," appears in *New Left Review* 181 (May–June 1990), 95–118. This absurdist exercise in historical social construction should be read in conjunction with Shelby Steele, *The Content of our Character* (New York, 1990), another piece of Negro intellectual delirium.

47. Eugene D. Genovese, *In Red and Black* (1968; Knoxville, 1984), 57. Genovese's attention to race in this essay differs from his analysis in *Roll, Jordan, Roll* (New York, 1972). In this important book Genovese treats race as class. After I wrote chapter 1 of this collection I read Eric Foner's splendid book *Reconstruction: America's Unfinished Revolution, 1863–1877* (New York, 1988). This book shows there is nothing inherent in a neo-Marxist analysis that precludes an examination of race as an autonomous factor in American history. The work I criticize in chapter 1 does not attempt such an examination. George M. Fredrickson's *The Arrogance of Race* (Middletown, Conn., 1988) does an excellent job of explicating the role of race in nineteenth-century America. When this book was in proofs I read Alexander Saxton's *The Rise and*

Fall of the White Republic (New York, 1990). This fine book also places race at the center of nineteenth-century American history.

48. Ibid.

49. Saul K. Padover, ed., *Karl Marx: On America and the Civil War* (New York, 1972), 275.

50. Hobsbawm, *Workers: Worlds of Labor*, 59.

51. On this point see Herbert Hill, "Race, Ethnicity, and Organized Labor: The Opposition to Affirmative Action," *New Politics* 1 (Winter 1987), 31–82; Mike Kazin, "Struggling with Class Struggle: Marxism and the Search for a Synthesis of U.S. *Labor History*," *Labor History* 28 (1987), 497–514; and David Roediger, "Labor in White Skin: Race and Working-Class History," in Davis and Sprinker, *Reshaping the U.S. Left*, 287–308.

52. Shlomo Avineri, ed., *Karl Marx on Colonialism and Modernization* (Garden City, N.Y., 1968), 10. See on this point the call for a re-thinking of class analysis by Leonard Harris, "Historical Subjects and Interest: Race, Class and Conflict," and Cornell West, "Race and Social Theory: Towards a Genealogical Materialist Analysis," both in Mike Davis, Manning Marable et al., eds., *The Year Left 2: An American Socialist Yearbook* (London, 1987), 90–105, 74–90; and Cornell West, "Marxist Theory and the Specificity of Afro-American Oppression," in Gary Nelson and Lawrence Grossberg, eds., *Marxism and the Interpretation of Culture* (Urbana, Ill., 1988), 17–29.

53. George Fredrickson, *The Black Image in the White Mind* (New York, 1971); Leon Litwack, *North of Slavery* (Chicago, 1961).

54. Carl Degler, *Neither Black nor White* (New York, 1971).

55. Fields, "Ideology and Race," 143. This criticism was also made of this essay by some members of the University of California Seminar in Southern History at U.C. Irvine on May 26, 1988.

56. Barbara J. Fields, *Slavery and Freedom on the Middle Ground* (New Haven, Conn., 1985); Hahn, *Roots of Southern Populism*; Lawrence Goodwyn, *The Populist Moment* (New York, 1978); Armistead L. Robinson, "Beyond the Realm of Social Consensus: New Meanings of Reconstruction for American History," *The Journal of American History* 68 (1981), 276–97; Jonathan Wiener, *Social Origins of the New South* (Baton Rouge, 1978), and "Class Structure and Economic Development in the American South," *American Historical Review* 84 (1979), 970–92.

57. For the problem of continuity in southern history see James C. Cobb, "Beyond Planters and Industrialists: A New Perspective on the New South," *The Journal of Southern History* 54 (1988), 45–68.

58. Jacob Katz, *From Persecution to Destruction: Anti-Semitism,*

1700–1933 (New York, 1978); Alfred D. Low, *Jews in the Eyes of the Germans* (Philadelphia, 1979); Michael A. Marrus, *The Politics of Assimilation* (Oxford, Eng., 1971).

59. See *The New York Times*, December 28, 1988; December 29, 1988; December 30, 1988; January 1, 1989; January 4, 1989; January 5, 1989; January 8, 1989; January 10, 1989; January 25, 1989; January 31, 1989. See also the story in *Jet* magazine for August 15, 1988, pp. 36–37. This story deals with the marketing of racist dolls in Japan. For an excellent discussion of the persistance of cultural attitudes before and after revolution see Judith Stacey, *Patriarchy and Socialist Revolution in China* (Berkeley, Calif., 1983). China was a partriarchial society before the Communist came to power in 1949 and continued to be one after the revolution. In short, women continued to be objectified and exploited after the establishment of the socialist republic.

60. Hiroshi Wagatsuma, "The Social Perception of Skin Color in Japan," *Daedalus* (1967), 407.

61. Ibid., 415.

62. Ibid., 435.

63. Fields, "Ideology and Race;" Peter Kolchin, *Unfree Labor* (Cambridge, Mass., 1988), 186.

64. George De Vos and Hiroshi Wagatsuma, *Japan's Invisible Race* (Berkeley, Calif., 1972), introduction, xx.

65. Ibid.

66. Ibid., 4.

67. See the exchange of letters on Judith Stein's book about Garvey in *The Journal of American History* 75 (1988), 324–27.

68. *The New York Times Book Review*, April 13, 1986. See also Wilson Jeremiah Moses, *Black Messiahs and Uncle Toms* (University Park, Pa., 1982), 124–41, and Judith Stein, *The World of Marcus Garvey* (Baton Rouge, 1986).

69. Lawrence W. Levine, "Marcus Garvey and the Politics of Revitalization," in John Hope Franklin and August Meier, eds., *Black Leaders of the Twentieth Century* (Urbana, Ill., 1982), 105–38. See the article by Salim Muwakkil, "Marcus Garvey," *In These Times*, September 10–16, 1986. See also the incidents of violence cited by Stein, *The World of Marcus Garvey*, 165–66 and 185.

70. Garvey's antipathy to folk culture was fairly common among members of his class in the West Indies. C.L.R. James in his study of cricket notes that his mother disapproved of his interest in calypso. See C.L.R. James, *Beyond a Boundary* (New York, 1983), 25–26.

71. Levine, "Marcus Garvey and the Politics of Revitalization," 116.

72. Meier and Rudwick, *Black History*, ch. 1. See also the fifth chapter of this book.

73. J. Saunders Redding, *On Being Negro in America* (Indianapolis, 1962).

74. Ibid., 40. Emory J. Tolbert, *The UNIA and Black Los Angeles* (Los Angeles, 1980), is an interesting study of the Garvey movement on the local level. The book tells us more about the leaders of the UNIA than it does about the common people who were drawn in Garveyism in Los Angeles.

75. Letter to Clarence E. Walker, October 21, 1984, in my possession.

76. For a thoughtful criticism of Genovese's analysis of slave religion see John Jentz, "A Note on Genovese's Account of the Slave's Religion," *Civil War History* 23 (1977), 161–69.

Chapter 1
How Many Niggers Did Karl Marx Know?

1. See, for example, Steven Hahn, *The Roots of Southern Populism* (New York, 1983); Barbara J. Fields, "Ideology and Race in American History," in J. Morgan Kousser and James M. McPherson, eds., *Region, Race, and Reconstruction* (New York, 1982), 143–77, and *Slavery and Freedom in the Middle Ground* (New Haven, Conn., 1985); Lawrence Goodwyn, "Populist Dreams and Negro Rights: East Texas as a Case Study," *American Historical Review* 76 (December 1971), 1435–56, and *The Populist Movement* (New York, 1978): Armistead L. Robinson, "Beyond the Realm of Social Consensus: New Meanings of Reconstruction for American History" *The Journal of American History* 68 (1981), 276–97; Jonathan Wiener, *Social Origins of the New South* (Baton Rouge, 1978), and "Class Structure and Economic Development in the American South," *American Historical Review* 84 (1979), 970–92.

2. Hahn, *The Roots of Southern Populism*, 90.

3. Robinson, "Beyond the Realm of Social Consensus," 285.

4. See Edmund L. Drago, *Black Politicians and Reconstruction in Georgia* (Baton Rouge, 1982), chs. 2 and 3. This fine book does an excellent job of placing race at the center of Reconstruction politics.

5. Robinson, "Beyond the Realm of Social Consensus," 285.

6. Fields, "Ideology and Race," 143.

7. Charles L. Flynn, Jr., *White Land, Black Labor* (Baton Rouge, 1983), 152 and 155.

8. Theodore Rosengarten, *All God's Dangers: The Life of Nate Shaw* (New York, 1974), 117.

9. What I call the "peculiar circumstances" of black life are examined in the following works, among others: Eric Anderson, *Race and Politics in North Carolina 1872–1901* (Baton Rouge, 1981); Edward L. Ayers, *Vengeance and Justice* (New York, 1981); Ira Berlin, *Slaves without Masters* (New York, 1974); Rowland Berthoff, "Conventional Mentality: Free Blacks, Women, and Business Corporations as Unequal Persons, 1820–1870," *The Journal of American History* 76 (December 1989), 753–84; Eugene Berwanger, *The Frontier against Slavery* (Urbana, Ill., 1967); Howard H. Bell, ed., *Proceedings of the National Negro Conventions, 1830–1864* (1830–64; New York, 1969); R.J.M. Blackett, *Beating against the Barriers* (Baton Rouge, 1986); David W. Blight, *Frederick Douglass's Civil War* (Baton Rouge, 1988); Joseph Boskin, *Sambo* (New York, 1986); Edmund L. Drago, *Black Politicians and Reconstruction in Georgia*; Don Fehrenbacher, *The Dred Scott Case* (New York, 1978); Eric Foner, *Reconstruction: America's Unfinished Revolution, 1863–1877*; George Fredrickson, *The Black Image in the White Mind* (New York, 1971); "Masters and Mudsills: The Role of Race in the Planter Ideology of South Carolina," in Jack R. Censer and W. Steven Steinert, eds., *South Atlantic Urban Studies* (Columbia, S.C., 1978), 34–48; *The Arrogance of Race*; Raymond Gavins, "The Meaning of Freedom: Black North Carolina in the Nadir, 1880–1900," in Jeffrey J. Crow, Paul D. Escott, and Charles L. Flynn, Jr., eds., *Race, Class and Politics in Southern History: Essays in Honor of Robert F. Durden* (Baton Rouge, 1989), 175–215; Elizabeth Fox-Genovese, *Within the Plantation Household*; Joseph T. Glatthar, *Forged in Battle* (New York, 1990); Calvin C. Hernton, *Sex and Racism in America* (New York, 1966); Leon A. Higginbotham, Jr., *In the Matter of Color* (New York, 1978); Reginald Horseman, *Josiah Nott* (Baton Rouge, 1987); Jacqueline Jones, *Labor of Love, Labor of Sorrow* (New York, 1985); Winthrop D. Jordan, *White over Black* (Chapel Hill, N.C., 1968); Roger Lane, *Roots of Violence in Black Philadelphia, 1860–1900* (Cambridge, Mass., 1981); Paul Lewinson, *Race, Class and Party* (1931; New York, 1965); Leon Litwack, *North of Slavery* (Chicago, 1961) and *Been in the Storm So Long* (New York, 1979); "Trouble in Mind: The Bicentennial and the Afro-American Experience," *Journal of American History* 74 (September 1987), 315–37; Edgar J. McManus, *Black*

Bondage in the North (Syracuse, N.Y., 1973); Neil R. McMillen, *Dark Journey* (Urbana, Ill., 1989); I.A. Newby, *Plain Folk in the New South* (Baton Rouge, 1989); James Oakes, *Slavery And Freedom: An Interpretation of the Old South* (New York, 1990); Nell I. Painter, *Exodusters* (New York, 1977); Bruce Palmer, *Man over Money* (Chapel Hill, N.C., 1980); Peter J. Parish, *Slavery: History and Historians* (New York, 1989); Jane H. Pease and William H. Pease, *They Who Would Be Free* (New York, 1974); Roger L. Ransom, *Conflict and Compromise: The Political Economy of Slavery, Emancipation, and the American Civil War* (Cambridge, Mass., 1989); Leonard Sweet, *Black Images of America, 1784–1870* (New York, 1976); William Stanton, *The Leopard's Spots* (Chicago, 1960); William L. Van De burg, *Slavery and Race in American Popular Culture* (Madison, Wisc., 1984); V. Jacque Vogeli, *Free but Not Equal* (Chicago, 1967); Clarence E. Walker, *A Rock in a Weary Land* (Baton Rouge, 1982); Joel Williamson, *After Slavery* (Chapel Hill, N.C., 1965), *New People* (New York, 1980), *The Crucible of Race* (New York, 1984); Charles H. Wesley, *Negro Labor in the United States* (1927; New York, 1967); and *Richard Allen* (Washington, D.C., 1935); Deborah G. White, *Arn't I a Woman?* (New York, 1985); Arthur Zilversmit, *The First Emancipation* (Chicago, 1967).

10. Robert Blauner, *Racial Oppression in America* (New York, 1972), 145–46. On this point see also Paul D. Escott, *Slavery Remembered* (Chapel Hill, N.C., 1979), 97.

11. Quoted in Rosengarten, *All God's Dangers*, 116.

12. For a discussion of this problem see ch. 5, this volume.

13. Whitelaw, Reid, *After the War*, C. Vann Woodward, ed. (1866; New York, 1965), 243.

14. David Potter, *People of Plenty* (Chicago, 1961), 29–30.

15. Marx, in the two books he co-authored with Frederick Engels, ignored the question of race. See Karl Marx and Frederick Engels, *Ireland and the Irish Question* (1843–94; New York, 1975), and *The First Indian War of Independence, 1857–1859* (1857–59; Moscow, 1975). For an interesting discussion of race in Marx's work see *Sociological Theories: Race and Colonialism* (Poole, Eng., 1980), Introductory Notes, 19–20 and 22. The racial aspect of the Sepoy Mutiny is discussed in Thomas Metcalf, *The Aftermath of Revolt* (Princeton, N.J., 1964).

16. *The Karl Marx Library*, Saul K. Padover, ed., vol. 2, *On America and the Civil War* (New York, 1972), 13.

17. Ambrose Bierce, *The Devil's Dictionary* (Mount Vernon, Va., 1958), 49.

18. Quoted in Van De burg, *Slavery and Race in American Popular Culture*, 28.

19. Fields, "Ideology and Race," 151.

20. Ibid., 143.

21. Ibid., 144.

22. Carl Degler, *Neither Black nor White*, and *Place over Time* (Baton Rouge, 1977); Fredrickson, *The Black Image*; Jordan, *White over Black*; Litwack, *North of Slavery*, and *Been in the Storm So Long*; Michael Rogin, *Fathers and Children* (New York, 1975); Richard Slotkin, *Regeneration through Violence* (Middletown, Conn., 1973), and *The Fatal Environment*; Joel Williamson, *The Crucible of Race*.

23. George Stocking, *Race, Culture, and Evolution* (New York, 1968), chs. 8 and 9. See also Ashley Montague, *Man's Most Dangerous Myth: The Fallacy of Race* (New York, 1974) For the genesis of Boas's interest in the Negro problem see Marshall Hyatt, "Franz Boas and the Struggle for Black Equality: The Dynamics of Ethnicity," *Perspectives in American History*, new series, 2 (1985), 269–95. See Harvard Sitkoff, *A New Deal for Blacks* (New York, 1978), ch. 8. See also Thomas F. Gossett, *Race: The History of an Idea in America* (New York, 1965), ch. 16.

24. See, for example, William B. Cohen, *The French Encounter with Africans* (Bloomington, Ind., 1980); Sander Gilman, *On Blackness without Blacks* (Boston, 1982); James Walvin, *Black and White: The Negro and English Society, 1555–1945* (London, 1973). I cite the Walvin book because it indicates that although the nineteenth-century black population of England was negligible, the English had begun to think that Negroes posed a threat to their society. For an interesting discussion of English racism see Errol Lawrence, "Just Plain Common Sense: The 'Roots' of Racism," in *The Empire Strikes Back* (London, 1982), 47–84.

25. Mike Davis, "Why the American Working Class Is Different," *Against the Current* 1, no. 2 (Winter 1981), 36–49, and *Prisoners of the American Dream* (London, 1986).

26. Sean Wilentz, "Against Exceptionalism: Class Consciousness and the American Labor Movement, 1790–1920," *International Labor and Working Class History* 26 (1984), 1–24. See also Michael Denning, "The Special American Conditions," Marxism and American Studies, *American Quarterly* 38 (1986), 357–80.

27. Republicanism's various manifestations are discussed in "Special Issue: Republicanism in the History and Historiography of the United States," *American Quarterly* 37 (1985).

28. For an interesting critique of "republicanism" see John P. Diggins, "Comrades and Citizens: New Methodologies in American Historiography," *American Historical Review* 90 (1985), 614–38.

29. W.E.B. DuBois, *Dusk of Dawn* (1940; New York, 1968), 205.

30. Michael Banton, *The Idea of Race* (London, 1977), ch. 1; Marvin Harris, *The Rise of Anthropological Theory* (New York, 1968), 87–93; and John C. Nott and George R. Glidden, *Types of Mankind* (Philadelphia, 1854).

31. Banton, *The Idea of Race*, ch. 1; Harris, *The Rise of Anthropological Theory*, 87–93; and Nott and Glidden, *Types of Mankind*.

32. Quoted in Banton, *The Idea of Race*, 2.

33. Thomas Jefferson, *Notes on the State of Virginia* (1861; New York, 1964), 138. For a brilliant discussion of Jefferson's Negro problem see Winthrop Jordan, *White over Black*, 429–81.

34. Iver Bernstein, *The New York City Draft Riots* (New York, 1990), David A. Carlton, *Mill and Town in South Carolina, 1880–1920* (Baton Rouge, 1982); Fields, *Slavery and Freedom on the Middle Ground*; Eugene D. Genovese, *Roll, Jordan, Roll*; Michael Fitzgerald, "Radical Republicanism and the White Yeomanry During Alabama Reconstruction, 1865–1868," *The Journal of Southern History* 54 (November 1988), 565–96, *The Union League Movement in the Deep South* (Baton Rouge, 1989); Herbert G. Gutman, *Work, Culture, and Society in Industrializing America* (New York, 1976); Hahn, *The Roots of Southern Populism*; J. Morgan Kousser, *The Shaping of Southern Politics, 1880–1910* (New Haven, Conn., 1974); David Montgomery, *Beyond Equality*; Peter J. Rachleff, *Black Labor in the South: Richmond, Virginia, 1865–1890* (Philadelphia, 1984); Wilentz, *Chants Democratic*. For a lively critique of the emphasis on class in American labor history see Herbert Hill, "Race, Ethnicity and Organized Labor: The Opposition to Affirmative Action," *New Politics* 1, no. 2 (Winter 1987), 31–82. See also the critiques of this article by David Brody, Dave Roedinger, and Nick Salvatore in *New Politics* 1, no. 3 (Summer 1987), 22–71.

35. Kousser, *The Shaping of Southern Politics*, passim.

36. Fernand Braudel, *On History* (Chicago, 1980), 27.

37. Quoted in Boskin, *Sambo*, 87.

38. George Mosse, *Toward the Final Solution* (New York, 1978).

39. Eric L. McKitrick, *Slavery Defended* (Englewood, Cliffs, N.J., 1963), 139 and 145.

40. Reverend H. Easton, "A Treatise on the Intellectual Character,

and Civil and Political Condition of the Colored People of the United States; And the Prejudice Exercised toward Them," in Dorothy Porter, ed., *Negro Protest Pamphlets* (1837; New York, 1969), 40.

41. Ibid., 41.

42. Ibid., 42.

43. Edgar T. Thompson, *Plantation Societies, Race Relations, and the South: The Regimentation of Populations* (Durham, N.C., 1975), chs. 4 and 5.

44. Leonard Richards, *Gentlemen of Property and Standing* (New York, 1970), passim; David H. Fowler, "Northern Atitudes towards Interracial Marriage: A Study of Legislation and Public Opinion in the Middle Atlantic States and States of the Old Northwest" (Ph.D. diss., Yale University, 1963); Sander Gilman, *Difference and Pathology* (Ithaca, N.Y., 1985), chs. 3 and 5.

45. Josiah Priest, *Slavery as It Relates to the Negro, or African Race* (1843; New York, 1977), 244. See also Henry Clay, "On African Colonization" in *The Life and Speeches of Henry Clay* (New York, 1843), 274.

46. Quoted in Voegeli, *Free But Not Equal*, 8.

47. Quoted in Fowler, "Northern Attitudes towards Interracial Marriage," 57.

48. Ibid., 11.

49. Ibid., 44. See also William G. Allen *The American Prejudice against Color* (1853; New York, 1969). Allen was a black man who married a white woman despite the objections of her family and community. Allen's pamphlet also contains a very poignant discussion of the discrimination suffered by free Negroes. "Reader, the life of a colored man in America, save as a slave," Allen says, "is regarded as far less sacred than a dog," 38.

50. Mary Douglas, *Purity and Danger* (Boston, 1966), 35.

51. Jordan, *White over Black*, 542.

52. J.H. Van Everie, *White Supremacy and Negro Subordination* (New York, 1868), 152.

53. Hernton, *Sex and Racism*, 90.

54. William Acton, *The Functions and Disorders of the Reproductive Organs in Youth, in Adult Age, and in Advanced Life: Considered in Their Social and Psychological Relations* (Philadelphia, 1858), 30; Jordan, *White over Black*, 34–35, 158–59; *The Papers of Frederick Law Olmstead,* Charles E. Beveridge and Charles Capen McLaughlin, eds., vol. 2, *Slavery and the South, 1852–57* (Baltimore, 1981); White, *Arn't*

I a Woman?, ch. 1. For a twentieth-century description of a Negro penis, see Milton A. McLaurin, *Separate Pasts* (Athens, Ga., 1987), 67.

55. Quoted in Arthur Calhoun, *A Social History of the American Family from Colonial Times to the Present* 2 (1919; New York, 1945), 249. See also pp. 3 and 53.

56. See Harriet Jacobs, *Incidents in the Life of a Slave Girl*; ed. Jean Fagan Yellin (1861; Cambridge, 1987) for an analysis of this problem. See also Jordan, *White over Black*, 151.

57. The concept of passionlessness is examined in Nancy F. Cott, "Passionlessness," in Nancy Cott and Elizabeth Pleck, ed., *A Heritage of Her Own* (New York, 1980), 162-81.

58. Bertram Wyatt-Brown, *Southern Honor* (New York, 1982), ch. 9; Catherine Clinton, *The Plantation Mistress* (New York, 1982); Irving H. Bartlett and C. Glenn Cambor, "The History and Psychodynamics of Southern Womanhood," *Women's Studies* 2 (1974), 9-24; Fox-Genovese, *Within the Plantation Household*, passim; Jacquelyn Dowd Hall, *Revolt against Chivalry* (New York, 1979); Anne Firor Scott, *The Southern Lady* (Chicago, 1970). See also Florence King, *Confessions of a Failed Southern Lady* (New York, 1985). This wonderful book adds new meaning to the phrase "cultural critique."

59. Bartlett and Cambor, "The History and Psychodynamics of Southern Womanhood," 11.

60. Wilbur J. Cash, *The Mind of the South* (New York, 1941), 38-39, 66, 83-87, 114-17.

61. James Weldon Johnson, *Along this Way* (1933; New York, 1986), 170.

62. Ibid.

63. Carroll Smith-Rosenberg, "Sex as Symbol in Victorian Purity: An Ethnohistorical Analysis of Jacksonian America," in John Demos and Sarane Spence Boocock, eds. *Turning Points* (Chicago, 1978) 212-47; Charles E. Rosenberg, "Sexuality, Class, and Role," in *No Other Gods* (Baltimore, 1976), 71-88; Ronald G. Walters, *The Antislavery Appeal* (Baltimore, 1976), ch. 5.

64. Jordan, *White over Black*, 141.

65. Violence directed at northern black people and their white allies is explored in the following works: Michael Feldberg, *The Turbulent Era* (New York, 1980); Emma Jones Lapansky, "'Since They Got Those Separate Churches': Afro-Americans and Racism In Jacksonian Philadelphia," *American Quarterly* 32 (1980), 54-78; Bruce Laurie, *Working People of*

Philadelphia (Philadelphia, 1980); Litwack, *North of Slavery*; Leonard L. Richards, *Gentlemen of Property and Standing* (New York, 1970); Richard C. Wade, "The Negro in Cincinnati, 1800-1830," in Dwight W. Hoover, ed., *Understanding Negro History* (Chicago, 1968), 126-37.

66. Berlin, *Slaves without Masters*; Leonard P. Curry, *The Free Black in Urban America, 1800-1850* (Chicago, 1981); Roark and Johnson, *Black Masters* (New York, 1984).

67. C. Vann Woodward, *The Strange Career of Jim Crow*, 3rd ed. (New York, 1974), 13-14. See also Howard Rabinowitz, *Race Relations in the Urban South* (New York, 1978); and Richard C. Wade, *Slavery in the Cities* (Chicago: 1964).

68. Litwack, *North of Slavery*, passim.

69. Alexis de Tocqueville, *Democracy in America*, J. P. Mayer, ed. (1848; Garden City, N.Y., 1968), part 1: 343.

70. Ray Allen Billington, ed., *The Journal of Charlotte L. Forten* (1854-64; New York, 1953), 68.

71. Ibid., 102-103.

72. *Colored American*, February 23, 1839.

73. Samuel Ringgold Ward, *Autobiography of a Fugitive Negro* (1855; New York, 1968), 283-84.

74. Quoted in Hollis R. Lynch, *Edward Wilmot Blyden* (New York, 1967), 28-29. See also Phillip S. Foner, ed., *The Life and Writings of Frederick Douglass*, 4 vols. (New York, 1955), 1: 319.

75. Degler, *Neither Black nor White*, ch. 5. See also Peter Kolchin, *Unfree Labor* (Cambridge, Mass., 1987), 187-88.

76. Foner, *The Life and Writings of Frederick Douglass*, 2: 224.

77. Ibid., 1: 319 and 235. See also Bell, ed., *Proceedings of the National Negro Conventions, 1830-1864*, passim.

78. Foner, *The Life and Writings of Frederick Douglass*, 1: 320.

79. Waldo Martin, *The Mind of Frederick Douglass* (Chapel Hill, N.C., 1984), 119. This aspect of nineteenth-century black thought is explored in Frederick Cooper, "Elevating the Race: The Social Thought of Black Leaders, 1827-1850," *American Quarterly* 24 (1972), 604-25; Leonard Sweet, *Black Images of America, 1784-1870* (New York, 1976); Walker, *A Rock in a Weary Land*, ch. 1.

80. Sweet, *Black Images of America*, 92-109.

81. W.E.B. DuBois, *The Philadelphia Negro*, 26-27; Laurie, *Working People of Philadelphia, 1800-1850*, 62-66; Lane, *Roots of Violence in Black Philadelphia, 1860-1900*, 18.

82. Quoted in Curry, *The Free Black in Urban America, 1800-1850*, 19.

83. Quoted in Carter G. Woodson, *The Mind of the Negro as Reflected in Letters Written during the Crisis, 1800-1860* (Washington, D.C., 1926), 657.

84. Foner, *The Life and Writings of Frederick Douglass*, 2: 224.

85. On this point see Hill, "Race, Ethnicity and Organized Labor," passim.

86. Quoted in Lane, *Roots of Violence in Black Philadelphia*, 18.

87. Hill, "Race, Ethnicity and Organized Labor," passim.

88. Ward, *Autobiography of a Fugitive Negro*, 38.

89. David A. Gerber, *Black Ohio and the Color Line, 1860-1915* (Urbana, Ill., 1976), 103-104.

90. Dale T. Knobel, *Paddy and the Republic* (Middletown, Conn., 1986), 100.

91. Ibid., 11.

92. Ibid., 38.

93. Quoted in ibid., 15.

94. Ibid., 88.

95. Ibid., 99.

96. Quoted in Banton, *The Idea of Race*, 87, n26.

97. L. Perry Curtis, Jr., *Apes and Angels: The Irishman in Victorian Caricature* (Washington, D.C., 1971), 29; *Anglo-Saxons and Celts: A Study of Anti-Irish Prejudice in Victorian England* (Bridgeport, Conn., 1968), 61.

98. Gilbert Osofsky, "Abolitionists, Irish Immigrants and the Dilemmas of Romantic Nationalism," *American Historical Review* 80 (1985), 889-912.

99. Banton, *The Idea of Race*, 3.

100. Ward, *Autobiography of a Fugitive Negro*, 382-83.

101. Fields, "Ideology and Race," 165; Peter Kolchin, *Unfree Labor: American Slavery and Russian Serfdom*, 186.

102. Quoted in Slotkin, *The Fatal Environment*, 481.

103. Quoted in Litwack, *Been in the Storm So Long*, 224.

104. Eric Foner, *Nothing But Freedom* (Baton Rouge, 1983).

105. Ida Wells Barnett made this point in her *On Lynchings* (1892, 1895, 1900; New York, 1969). See p. 20 of the essay "Southern Horrors." Bertram Doyle, *The Etiquette of Race Relations* (1937; New York, 1971), p. xxviii. C. Vann Woodward in *Thinking Back* (Baton Rouge, 1986) disputes the idea of continuity in southern history. See ch. 4.

106. John Blassingame, *The Slave Community*; Ulrich B. Phillips, *American Negro Slavery* (1918; Baton Rouge, 1966); Kenneth M. Stampp, *The Peculiar Institution* (New York, 1956).

107. Berlin, *Slave without Masters*; Roark and Johnson, *Black Masters*.

108. For the problem of Jewish emancipation see the following works: Jacob Katz, "The German Jewish Utopia of Social Emancipation," in Max Kreutzberger, ed., *Studies of the Leo Baeck Institute* (New York, 1967), 60–80; *Out of the Ghetto: The Social Background of Jewish Emancipation, 1770–1870* (New York, 1978); and *From Persecution to Destruction: Anti-Semitism, 1700–1933* (New York, 1978); Michael R. Marrus, *The Politics of Assimilation* (Oxford, Eng., 1971); Reinhard Rurrup, "Jewish Emancipation and Bourgeois Society," *Leo Baeck Institute Yearbook* 14 (1969), 67–91; "German Liberalism and the Emancipation of the Jews," *Leo Baeck Institute Yearbook* 20 (1975), 59–69.

109. Katz, *From Persecution to Destruction*, 103 and 226.

110. Sidney Andrews, *The South since the War* (1866; New York, 1969), 398; Walter L. Fleming, *Documentary History of Reconstruction*, 2 vols. (1906–1907; Gloucester, Mass., 1960), 1: 251 and 2: 398.

111. Andrews, *The South since the War*, 87; John R. Dennett, *The South As It Is, 1865–1866*, Henry M. Christian, ed. (1865–66; New York, 1965), 349.

112. Andrews, *The South since the War*, 100.

113. Myrta Avary, *Dixie after the War* (1906; Boston, 1937), 203.

114. Quoted in Thomas Holt, *Black over White* (Urbana, Ill., 1977), 25.

115. Quoted in Litwack, *North of Slavery*, 53.

116. Myrta Avary, ed., *Recollections of Alexander H. Stephens* (New York, 1907), 207.

117. Dennett, *The South As It Is*, 41, 84, and 328; Whitelaw Reid, *After the War*, C. Vann Woodward, ed. (1866; New York, 1965), 84.

118. Dennett, *The South As It Is*, 129.

119. Ulrich B. Phillips, "The Central Theme of Southern History," *American Historical Review* 34 (1928), 30–48.

120. Degler, *Time over Place*, passim; Litwack, *Been in the Storm So Long*, passim; and Dan T. Carter, *When the War Was Over* (Baton Rouge, 1985), ch. 5.

121. For a provocative but unconvincing effort to make class conflict, not race, the central issue of Reconstruction, see Armistead L. Robinson, "Beyond the Realm of Social Consensus: New Meanings of Reconstruction for American History."

122. In her essay "Ideology and Race in American History" Barbara Fields calls white supremacy a "slogan" and ignores its broader repercussions. For evidence that white supremacy was more than just a slogan, see Guion G. Johnson, "The Ideology of White Supremacy, 1876–1910," in Fletcher Green, ed., *Essays in Southern History* 31 (Chapel Hill, N.C., 1949), 124–56; James W. Vander Zanden, "The Ideology of White Supremacy," *Journal of the History of Ideas* 20 (1959), 385–402.

123. See A.T. Morgan, *Yazoo; or on the Picket Line of Freedom in the South* (Washington, D.C., 1894), passim.

124. Dennett, *The South As It Is*, 31.

125. Fleming, *Documentary History of Reconstruction*, 1: 274 and 286; 2: 288–289 and 291.

126. On this point, see Doyle, *The Etiquette of Race Relations,* 123.

127. Reid, *After the War*, 318.

128. Ibid., 359.

129. Quoted in Fields, *Slavery and Freedom on the Middle Ground*, 125.

130. Doyle, *The Etiquette of Race Relations*, 109.

131. Ibid., 14.

132. Ibid., 54.

133. Fredrick Bancroft, ed., *Speeches, Correspondence and Political Papers of Carl Schurz* (New York, 1913), 1: 34.

134. The first quotation in this sentence is from Doyle, *The Etiquette of Race Relations*, 118. The second quotation comes from Dennett, *The South As It Is*, 42.

135. Andrews, *The South since the War*, 187.

136. Dennett, *The South As It Is*, 132 and 270.

137. Williamson, *The Crucible of Race*, 319.

138. Barnett, *On Lynchings*, passim; Doyle, *The Etiquette of Race Relations*, 120.

139. Dennett, *The South As It Is*, 96.

140. Reid, *After the War*, 363.

141. Dennett, *The South As It Is*, 169.

142. Ibid., 368.

143. See note 1, above.

144. Wiener, "Class Structure and Economics in the American South, 1865–1955."

145. Ibid., 978.

146. Flynn, *White Land, Black Labor*, 151–52; Enoch Spencer Sim-

mons, *A Solution of the Race Problem in the South* (Raleigh, N.C., 1898), 24–25.

147. Fields, "Ideology and Race," 156 and 157.

148. Ibid.; Hahn, *The Roots of Southern Populism*, 109; Robinson, "Beyond the Realm of Social Consensus," passim.

149. Dennett, *The South As It Is*, 119.

150. Andrews, *The South since the War*, 396.

151. Fleming, *Documentary History of Reconstruction*, 1: 81.

152. Ibid., 338.

153. Quoted in Samuel Hynes, "A Little Cockney Cad," *The New Republic*, May 28, 1984, p. 32.

154. Kousser, *The Shaping of Southern Politics* (New Haven, Conn., 1974), 36.

155. C. Vann Woodward, *Tom Watson, Agrarian Rebel* (New York, 1938), *Origins of the New South* (Baton Rouge, 1951), *Reunion and Reaction* (Boston, 1956), *The Strange Career of Jim Crow* (New York, 1955), and *Thinking Back*. See also the assessment of Woodward's work by George Fredrickson, "C. Vann Woodward, Renaissance of Southern History," *Dissent* (Winter 1987), 66–72.

156. Woodward, *Thinking Back*, ch. 4.

157. Woodward, *Origins of the New South*, 222.

158. Woodward, *Tom Watson*.

159. Ibid., 239–40. See Charles Crowe's critique of Woodward's book, "Tom Watson, Populist, and Blacks Reconsidered," *The Journal of Negro History* 55 (1970), 90–116.

160. Crowe, "Tom Watson, Populist, and Blacks Reconsidered;" Robert M. Saunders, "The Southern Populist and the Negro in 1892," in *University of Virginia Essays in History*, (Charlottesville, Va., 1966–67), 12: 7–25; "The Southern Populist and the Negro, 1893–1905," *Journal of Negro History* 54 (1969), 240–61; "The Transformation of Tom Watson, 1894–95," *Georgia Historical Quarterly* 34 (1970), 339–56. See also Gregg Cantrell and D. Scott Barton, *Texas Populists and the Failure of Biracial Politics, The Journal of Southern History* 55 (November 1989), 659–92.

161. Saunders, "The Populist and the Negro in 1892," 13 and 21; Barton Shaw, *The Wool-Hat Boys* (Baton Rouge, 1984), ch. 4. See also the statement by the president of the Southern Farmers' Alliance quoted in Michael Schwartz, *Radical Protest and Social Structure* (New York, 1976), 98. Vann Woodward's expectations of the Populists as racial reformers are muted in *The Origins of the New South*, 254. For a general critique

of the Populists as friends of the Negro, see Robert L. Allen, *Reluctant Reformers* (New York, 1975), ch. 3.

162. Shaw, *The Wool-Hat Boys*, 3.

163. Ibid., 79.

164. Simmons, *Solution to the Race Problem*, 29–30; A. T. Morgan, *Yazoo*, 211–12, 343–53, 455, 466.

165. Simmons, *Solution to the Race Problem*, 21.

166. Quoted in Shaw, *The Wool-Hat Boys*, 83. See also Bruce Palmer, *Man over Money*, for the following quotation taken from a Populist paper in 1896. The paper said "no negro was ever promised any political position by the Populists. . . . No Negro ever held a seat in any Populist convention in Alabama," 55 and 66.

167. Flemming, *Documentary History of Reconstruction*, 1:84–85; 2:275.

168. *Report of the Committee of the Senate Upon the Relations Between Labor and Capital*, 4 vols. (1885; New York, 1976), 4: 463.

169. Ibid., 4: 572 and 576.

170. Flemming, *Documentary History of Reconstruction*, 2: 446.

171. Booker T. Washington, *Up from Slavery* (1901; New York, 1986). For an interesting southern white critique of Booker T. Washington, see Thomas Dixon, Jr., "Booker T. Washington and the Negro," *Saturday Evening Post*, August 19, 1905, pp. 1–2.

172. Quoted in Marrus, *The Politics of Assimilation*, 175; see also 171–72 and 175.

173. Washington, *Up from Slavery*, 40–41. For Washington's life and career see Louis R. Harlan, *Booker T. Washington*, 2 vols. (New York, 1972 and 1983).

174. This problem is discussed in ch. 5, this volume.

175. Washington, *Up from Slavery*, 86. The best discussion of disfranchisement in the South is Kousser, *The Shaping of Southern Politics*, passim.

176. Reid, *After the War*, 318.

177. Williamson, *The Crucible of Race*, 178.

178. Barnett, *On Lynching*, 10–11.

179. Ibid., 18. See also William Archer, *Through Afro-America* (New York, 1910), 32, 33 and 137, and Maurice S. Evans, *Black and White in the Southern States* (New York, 1915), 32.

180. Barnett, *On Lynching*, 19.

181. Williamson, *The Crucible of Race*, 190.

182. *The Booker T. Washington Papers*, Louis R. Harland and Raymond W. Smock, eds. (Urbana, Ill., 1977), 7 (1903-4):62 and 70.

183. Katz, *From Persecution to Destruction: Anti-Semitism, 1700-1933*, 226.

184. Hahn, *The Roots of Southern Populism*, 109.

185. Sutton E. Griggs, *Wisdom's Call* (Nashville, 1911), 113.

186. Conversation with my colleague, Morton Rothstein.

187. See H.W. Velakazi, "Was Karl Marx a Black Man?" *Monthly Review* 32 (June 1980), 42-58.

Chapter 2
The Virtuoso Illusionist: Marcus Garvey

1. Alice Childress, *A Short Walk* (New York, 1979), 150-51.

2. Those historians who have accorded Garvey a heroic role in American black history are, I think, practicing a form of "Whig History," in which the interpretation of past events is dependent upon perceptions of present needs. For the concept of Whig History see Herbert Butterfield, *The Whig Interpretation of History* (New York, 1965). The following works are among those that depict Garvey and Garveyism in a heroic mold: Randall K. Burkett, *Garveyism as a Religious Movement* (Metuchen, N.J., 1978); *Black Redemption* (Philadelphia, 1978); John Henrik Clarke, ed., *Marcus Garvey and the Vision of Africa* (New York, 1973); Edmund David Cronon, *Black Moses* (Madison, Wisc., 1968); Adolph Edwards, *Marcus Garvey* (London, 1967); Elton G. Fax, *Garvey: The Story of a Pioneer Black Nationalist* (New York, 1972); John Hope Franklin, *From Slavery to Freedom: A History of Negro Americans*, 5th ed. (New York, 1979), 354-56; Richard Hart, "The Life and Resurrection of Marcus Garvey," *Race* 9 (October 1967): 217-37. See the introduction written by Robert A. Hill, ed., *The Marcus Garvey and Universal Negro Improvement Association Papers,* 6 vols., (Berkeley, Calif., 1980), 1:xxxv-xc; James Weldon Johnson, *Black Manhattan* (New York, 1930; Philadelphia, 1968); Lawrence W. Levine, "Marcus Garvey and the Politics of Revitalization," in John Hope Franklin and August Meier, eds., *Black Leaders of the Twentieth Century* (Urbana, Ill., 1982), 105-138; Tony Martin, *Race First* (Westport, Conn., 1976); Len S. Nembhard, *Trials and Triumphs of Marcus Garvey* (1940; Millwood, 1978); Roi Ottley, *New World A-Coming* (1943; New York, 1969), 68-81; Alphonso Pinkney, *Red, Black*

and Green: Black Nationalism in the United States (New York, 1976), 37–56; Theodore G. Vincent, *Black Power and the Garvey Movement* (New York, 1971); Robert G. Weisbord, *Ebony Kinship* (Westport, Conn., 1973), 51–89.

3. Cronon, *Black Moses*; Levine, "Marcus Garvey and the Politics of Revitalization;" Johnson, *Black Manhattan*, 256.

4. Quoted in Fax, *Garvey*, 99.

5. Harold Cruse, *The Crisis of the Negro Intellectual* (New York: Morrow, 1967), 124.

6. The best book-length study of the Garvey movement is Boyd C. James, "Primitives on the Move: Some Historical Articulations of Garvey and Garveyism, 1887–1927" (Ph.D. diss., University of California, Los Angeles, 1982).

7. Ibid., 24, n2.

8. Tony Martin, *Race First*, 23; George Padmore, *Pan-Africanism or Communism?* (Garden City, N.Y., 1972), 66. The reference to "black Negroes" is from Clarke, *Marcus Garvey*, 71.

9. For a detailed discussion of the concept of the "mulatto escape hatch," see Carl N. Degler, *Neither Black nor White* (New York, 1971), 205–64. See also Winthrop D. Jordan, *White over Black* (Chapel Hill, 1968), 167–78; C.L.R. James, *Beyond a Boundary* (New York, 1984), 57–58; David Lowenthal, "Race & Color in the West Indies," *Daedalus* (Spring 1967); 580–626; and Carl S. Mathews, "Marcus Garvey writes from Jamaica on the Mulatto Escape Hatch," *Journal of Negro History* 59 (April 1974):170–76.

10. Clarke, *Marcus Garvey*, 72.

11. Ibid.; James, "Primitives on the Move," 50–160; Amy Jacques-Garvey, *Garvey & Garveyism* (Kingston, Jamaica, 1963), 10.

12. James, "Primitives on the Move," 57–161; Cronon, *Black Moses*, 12–13.

13. Ibid.

14. Ibid., 13–14; James, "Primitives on the Move," 107–109.

15. Clarke, *Marcus Garvey*, 73.

16. Ibid.

17. James, "Primitives on the Move," 108–40.

18. Clarke, *Marcus Garvey*, 73.

19. See Lawrence W. Levine, "Marcus Garvey and the Politics of Revitalization," 109.

20. Robert A. Hill, "The First England Years and After, 1912–1916," in Clarke, *Marcus Garvey*, 59.

21. Ibid. For a nineteenth-century American Black expression of the idea of general racial improvement, see "Ten Letters by Augustine: Moral Work for Colored Men," in Sterling Stuckey, ed., *The Ideological Origins of Black Nationalism* (Boston, 1972), 121.

22. Quoted in Hill, *The Marcus Garvey and Universal Negro Improvement Association Papers*, 1:li. For the concept of nationalism, see Hans Kohn, *The Idea of Nationalism* (New York, 1944), 3–24.

23. Quoted in Hill, *The Marcus Garvey and Universal Negro Improvement Association Papers*, 1:li. In refusing to base his movement on folk cultural forms Garvey followed a fairly common practice among educated West Indians. For a discussion of this issue, see James, *Beyond a Boundary*, 26; and Lowenthal, "Race and Color in the West Indies," 593.

24. Quoted in Hill, "The First England Years and After, 1912–1916," 59.

25. Ibid.

26. Ibid., 65, 66.

27. Although much has been made of Garvey's admiration of Booker T. Washington, recent work suggests that the two men were not ideologically congruent. See, for example, Louis R. Harlan, *Booker T. Washington: The Wizard of Tuskegee, 1901–1915* (New York, 1983), 280–81.

28. The problem of black migration and its impact on American race relations is discussed in the following works: Cronon, *Black Moses*, 23; Floretti Henri, *Black Migration* (New York, 1976); David M. Kennedy, *Over Here* (New York, 1980); Gilbert Osofsky, *Harlem: The Making of a Ghetto Negro, New York, 1890–1930* (New York, 1977); Allan H. Spear, *Black Chicago* (Chicago, 1967).

29. Elliott Rudwick, *Race Riot at East St. Louis* (Urbana, Ill., 1982).

30. Cronon, *Black Moses*, 31.

31. Franklin, *From Slavery to Freedom*, 347.

32. Quoted in Arthur E. Barbeau and Floretti Henri, *The Unknown Soldier* (Philadelphia, 1974), 175.

33. Cronon, *Black Moses*, 36. See Levine, "Marcus Garvey and the Politics of Revitalization," passim; Martin, *Race First*; and Theodore G. Vincent, *Black Power and the Garvey Movement*.

34. Exactly how many followers Garvey had is difficult to ascertain. See the varying estimates given in the following works: Cronon, *Black Moses*, 205–206; Levine, "Marcus Garvey and the Politics of Revitalization," 121–22; and Martin, *Race First*, 13–17 and the appendix. Garvey

scholars are caught in the same numbers game as students of the African slave trade who, until Philip Curtin brought order out of chaos, were overestimating the number of slaves taken from Africa. See Philip Curtin, *The Atlantic Slave Trade: A Census* (Madison, Wisc., 1969), 3–13.

35. Levine, "Marcus Garvey and the Politics of Revitalization," 121.

36. Osofsky, *Harlem*, 43–45; Spear, *Black Chicago*, 147–68.

37. Ira De A. Reid, *The Negro Immigrant* (1939; New York, 1968).

38. David J. Hellwig, "Black Meets Black: Afro-American Reactions to West Indian Immigrants in the 1920," *South Atlantic Quarterly* 77 (Spring 1978), 209; Osofsky, *Harlem*, 131–35.

39. Hellwig, "Black Meets Black," 210–11.

40. Ibid.

41. Louis R. Harlan, "Booker T. Washington's Discovery of Jews" in J. Morgan Kousser and James M. McPherson, eds., *Region, Race, and Reconstruction* (New York, 1982), 267–79; Seth Shiner, *Negro Mecca* (New York, 1965), 130–33; Clarence E. Walker, *A Rock in a Weary Land: The African Methodist Episcopal Church during the Civil War and Reconstruction* (Baton Rouge, 1982), 111.

42. Hellwig, "Black Meets Black," passim; Osofsky, *Harlem*, 132; Reid, *The Negro Immigrant*, 152.

43. Quoted in Osofsky, *Harlem*, 133.

44. Ibid., 134.

45. Quoted in Hellwig, "Black Meets Black," 220.

46. Carl Freedman, "Over Determinations: on Black Marxism in Britain," *Social Text* 11 (Winter), 1983–84, 142.

47. Amy Jacques-Garvey, ed., *Philosophy and Opinions of Marcus Garvey*, 2 vols. (New York, 1969), 1:70–71; 2:40.

48. I want to thank Professor Ann Wightman for helping me formulate this point.

49. Marcus Garvey, *The Black Man*, 2 vols. (New York, 1975), December, 1933, 1:13.

50. Hans Rogger and Eugen Weber, eds., *The European Right* (Berkeley, Calif., 1966), 21. For a case study of the evolution of a specific racial myth see Hugh A. MacDouglas, *Racial Myth in English History* (Hanover, Mass., 1982).

51. Ibid.

52. Ibid., 22.

53. Quoted in Ibid.

54. Edwin S. Redkey makes this conflation in his essay "The Flower-

ing of Black Nationalism: Henry McNeal Turner and Marcus Garvey," in Nathan I. Huggins, Martin Kelson, and Daniel M. Fox, eds., *Key Issues in the Afro-American Experience*, 2 vols. (New York, 1971), 2:107–24. The most comprehensive study of antebellum black colonization and emigration is Floyd J. Miller, *The Search for a Black Nationality* (Urbana, Ill., 1975). This work, along with Wilson Jeremiah Moses, *The Golden Age of Black Nationalism 1850–1925* (Hamden, N.J., 1978), reveals a number of the tensions and contradictions present in nineteenth-century black nationalism.

55. Sheldon H. Harris, *Paul Cuffe, Black America, and the African Return* (New York, 1972); Howard A. Bell, ed., *Search for a Place* (Ann Arbor, Mich., 1969); Martin Robinson Delany, *The Condition, Elevation, Emigration, and Destiny of the Colored People of the United States* (1852; New York, 1968), 159–214.

56. Edwin S. Redkey, *Black Exodus* (New Haven, Conn., 1969), 195–96.

57. Amy Jacques-Garvey, *Philosophy and Opinions*, 2:122.

58. Ibid., 119.

59. Quoted in Amy Jacques-Garvey, *Garvey and Garveyism* (Kingston, Jamaica, 1963), 104.

60. Amy Jacques-Garvey, *Philosophy and Opinions*, 1:37. The intellectual underpinnings of Garvey's ideas about mulattoes were quite old. See Thomas F. Gossett, *Race: The History of an Idea in America* (New York, 1965), 49–50; Joel Williamson, *New People* (New York, 1980), 73; William Stanton, *The Leopard's Spots* (Chicago, 1960), 66–68.

61. W.E.B. DuBois, *The Souls of Black Folk* (1903; Greenwich, Conn., 1961), 23.

62. Amy Jacques-Garvey, *Philosophy and Opinions*, 1:41, 52.

63. Ibid., 1:40.

64. Ibid., 1:40–41.

65. Ibid., 2:5.

66. Marcus Garvey, *The Black Man*, February 1934, 1:6; Amy Jacques-Garvey, *Philosophy and Opinions*, 1:52.

67. Garvey, *The Black Man*, February 1934, I:6.

68. My understanding of Zionism and Herzl is derived from the following works: Shlomo Avineri, *The Making of Modern Zionism* (New York, 1981), 88–100, 159–86; Amos Elon, *The Israelis* (New York, 1983), Part I; Jacques Kornberg, "Theodore Herzl: A Reevaluation," *Journal of Modern History* 52 (June 1980), 226–52; Peter Lowenberg, *Decoding*

the Past (New York, 1983), 101–35; Carl E. Schorske, *Fin-de-Siècle Vienna* (New York, 1980), 116–80.

69. "Let Us Go into the House of the Lord," Century Records 31016.

70. Lowenberg, *Decoding the Past,* 121.

71. Kohn, *The Idea of Nationalism,* 16.

72. Garvey, *The Black Man,* December 1933, I:6.

73. George Steiner, "The Hollow Man," *The New Yorker,* August 30, 1982, p. 86. See also Susan Sontag's brilliant essay, "Fascinating Fascism," in *Under the Sign of Saturn* (New York, 1980), 73–105.

74. Ottley, *New World A-Coming,* 68–81.

75. Cronon, *Black Moses*; Levine, "Marcus Garvey and the Politics of Revitalization," passim.

76. Quoted in Amy Jacques-Garvey, *Garvey and Garveyism,* 65. See also the instructions on deportment Garvey gave his followers, in Tony Martin, ed., *Message to the People: The Course of African Philosophy* (Dover, Mass., 1986), passim.

77. Ibid.

78. Ibid., 103.

79. Hans Rogger and Eugen Weber, eds., *The European Right* (Berkeley, Calif., 1965), 27.

80. Jervis Anderson, *This Was Harlem, 1900–1950* (New York, 1981), 125; Cronon, *Black Moses,* 69–70. For the concept of identification with the aggressor see Anna Freud's insightful essay, *The Ego and the Mechanisms of Defense* (New York, 1971), 109–21.

81. Randall K. Burkett, *Garveyism as a Religious Movement: Black Redemption.* I have some problem accepting this argument. To say that Garveyism was a religious movement suggests that Garvey's followers thought of him as a god or God's messenger and makes critics of the movement heretics or apostates.

82. Quoted in Anderson, *A. Philip Randolph* (New York, 1972), 120–37; Martin, *Race First,* 143–43.

83. Quoted in Anderson, *A. Philip Randolph,* 132–33.

84. Amy Jacques-Garvey, *Philosophy and Opinions,* 1:57–64; 2:122–23.

85. Ibid., 2:41.

86. Ibid., 1:29.

87. Ibid., 1:56.

88. Ibid., 2:123.

89. Anderson, A. Philip Randolph, 127.

90. Amy Jacques-Garvey, *Philosophy and Opinions*, 2:310.

91. Ibid.

92. Hollis R. Lynch, *Edward Wilmot Blyden* (New York, 1967), 59, 135. See also Garvey's comments about George Schuyler in *The Black Man*, December 1933, 1:4; February 1934, 1:9.

93. Hollis R. Lynch, ed., *Selected Letters of Edward Wilmot Blyden* (Millwood, N.Y., 1978), 174–75, 372.

94. Amy Jacques-Garvey, *Philosophy and Opinions*, 2:43.

95. Garvey, *The Black Man,* February 1934, 1:2.

96. Amy Jacques-Garvey, *Philosophy and Opinions*, 2:72.

97. Ibid., 70.

98. Ibid.

99. Ibid., 70–71.

100. Ibid., 70.

101. Quoted in Cronon, *Black Moses*, 188.

102. Amy Jacques-Garvey, *Philosophy and Opinions*, 2:71.

103. Quoted in Reid, *The Negro Immigrant*, 153.

104. See, for example, the discussion of race and Jews in Sebastian Haffner, *The Meaning of Hitler*, trans. Ewald Osers (Cambridge, Mass., 1983), 80–82. In Garvey's thought, I would argue, mulattoes served the same function as Jews did in Hitler's ideology. Juan J. Linz, "Some Notes toward a Comparative Study of Fascism in Sociological Historical Perspective," in Walter Lacquer, ed., *Facism: A Reader's Guide* (Berkeley, Calif., 1978), 9, 12–13.

105. Judith Stein, "Pardon Marcus Garvey," *New York Times*, November 5, 1983. See also Stein's *The World of Marcus Garvey*, passim.

106. Jonathan Tasine, "The Rise and Fall of Marcus Garvey," *Los Angeles Times*, September 25, 1983.

107. Denis Mack Smith, *Mussolini* (New York, 1982), 252. See also Dennis Mack Smith's *Mussolini's Roman Empire* (New York, 1972). I would like to thank Professors Eugene Lunn, Barbara Metcalf, Rosalind Rosenberg, Nicholas Salvatore, Ronald Schatz, Richard Slotkin, Frank B. Tipton, Jerry Watts, and Ann Wightman for reading earlier drafts of this essay.

Chapter 3
Massa's New Clothes: A Critique of Eugene D. Genovese

This chapter was published previously as an article in *Umoja* 4, no. 2 (Summer 1980). It is used by permission.

1. John Blassingame, *The Slave Community* (New York, 1972); Stanley Elkins, *Slavery*, 3rd ed., rev. (Chicago, 1976); Robert W. Fogel and Stanley L. Engerman, *Time on the Cross: The Economics of American Negro Slavery*, 2 vols. (Boston, 1974); Herbert G. Gutman, *The Black Family in Slavery and Freedom 1750-1925* (New York, 1976); Nathan Huggins, *Black Odyssey* (New York, 1977); George P. Rawick, *From Sundown to Sunup* (Westport, Conn., 1972). Throughout this essay the terms "paradigm" and "conceptual framework" will be used interchangeably. For the use of the term paradigm and its implications for historical analysis, see David A. Hollinger's essay, "T.S. Kuhn's Theory of Science and Its Implications for History," *American Historical Review* 78 (April, 1973), 370-90. See also Thomas S. Kuhn's *The Structure of Scientific Revolutions*, 2nd ed., enlarged (Chicago, 1970). Though numerous historians have contributed to our understanding of the peculiar institution since 1956, no one has attempted a more forceful, thorough, stimulating alternative interpretation to Stampp than Genovese. It is therefore not suprising that *Roll, Jordan, Roll* has shaped current debates about slavery. This essay is a critical reading of *Roll, Jordan, Roll*. See also my critiques of the following works: Frank B. Tipton, Jr., and Clarence E. Walker, "Time on the Cross," *History and Theory* 14 (1975), pp. 91-121; Walker, "Black Bancroft," a review essay of *There Is a River, Journal of Ethnic Studies* 11 (1983), 111-18; *Slave Culture* is examined in "Three Books on Race," *Journal of American Ethnic History* 9 (Spring 1990), 79-84.

2. See, for example, Genovese's *The Political Economy of Slavery* (New York, 1965); *In Red and Black* (1968; Knoxville, 1984); *The World the Slaveholders Made* (New York, 1969); *Roll, Jordan, Roll* (New York, 1972).

3. For Gramsci's life and work see the following: John M. Cammett, *Antonio Gramsci and the Origins of Italian Communism* (Stanford, Conn., 1971); Giuseppi Fiori, *Antonio Gramsci: Life of a Revolutionary* (New York, 1973). The concept of hegemony is scattered throughout Gramsci's work. See, for example, Quentin Hoare and Geoffrey Nowell

Smith, eds., *Selections from the Prison Notebooks of Antonio Gramsci* (New York, 1971), passim. Perry Anderson's superb essay "The Antinomies of Antonio Gramsci," *New Left Review* 100 (Nov. 1976-Jan. 1977), 5-78, and Carl Boggs, *Gramsci's Marxism* (London, 1976) ch. 2; Joseph Femia, "Hegemony and Consciousness in the Thought of Antonio Gramsci," *Political Studies* 23 (1975), 29-48, have broadened my understanding of Gramsci and hegemony.

4. Gwyn A. Williams, "The Concept of Egemonia in the Thought of Antonio Gramsci: Some Notes on Interpretation," *Journal of the History of Ideas* 21 (Oct.-Dec. 1960), 586-99. The following comments about Gramsci are based on my reading of Anderson, "The Antinomies of Antonio Gramsci," passim; Boggs, *Gramsci's Marxism*, 39-40. See also Boggs's comments about Gramsci's understanding of slavery and black history in footnote 20, pages 131-32; and Femia, "Hegemony and Consciousness," 29-30.

5. Genovese, *The Political Economy of Slavery*, 3, 15-16, 28.

6. Ulrich B. Phillips, *American Negro Slavery* (1918; Baton Rouge, 1966); *Life and Labor in the Old South* (Boston, 1929).

7. Genovese, *Roll, Jordan, Roll*, 3.

8. Ibid., 5.

9. Boggs, *Gramsci's Marxism*, 39-40.

10. Genovese, *In Red and Black*, 407.

11. The following works contain material which suggests that the planters' hegemony was not as complete as Genovese has argued. Carl Degler, *The Other South* (New York, 1974), chs. 3, 4, 5; Clement Eaton, *Freedom of Thought in the Old South* (1940; Gloucester, Mass., 1951); *The Growth of Southern Civilization* (New York, 1961), 174-76; Fletcher M. Green, *Constitutional Development in the South Atlantic States, 1776-1860* (Chapel Hill, N.C., 1930); and "Democracy in the Old South," *Journal of Southern History* 12 (Feb. 1946), 3-23; Charles S. Sydnor, *The Development of Southern Sectionalism 1819-1848* (Baton Rouge, 1948), ch. 12; Ronald T. Takaki, *A Pro-Slavery Crusade* (New York, 1971), passim; J. Mills Thornton III, *Politics and Power in a Slave Society, Alabama, 1800-1860* (Baton Rouge, 1978), passim; Gavin Wright, *The Political Economy of the Cotton South* (New York, 1978), 37-42.

12. Leonardo Salamini, "Gramsci and Marxist Sociology of Knowledge: An Analysis of Hegemony—Ideology—Knowledge," *The Sociological Quarterly* 15 (Summer 1974), 370.

13. Eugene D. Genovese, "Yeoman Farmers in a Slaveholders' Democracy," *Agricultural History* 49 (April 1975), 331–42.

14. Ibid., 333.

15. Ibid., 340–51.

16. Harvey Wish, ed., *Ante-Bellum: Three Classic Works on Slavery, Writings of George Fitzhugh and Hinton Rowan Helper on Slavery* (1854, 1857; New York, 1960), 29.

17. Clement Eaton, *A History of the Southern Confederacy* (New York, 1954); Earl Schenck Miers, ed., *A Rebel War Clerk's Diary* (1866; New York, 1961); James L. Roark, *Masters without Slaves* (New York, 1977).

18. William W. Freehling, *Prelude to Civil War* (New York, 1965), ch. 3.

19. Russel B. Nye, *Fettered Freedom* (Urbana, Ill., 1972), 29–30; Stephen B. Oates, *The Fires of Jubilee* (New York, 1975), 99–100; C. Vann Woodward, *The Burden of Southern History* (Baton Rouge, 1960), ch. 3.

20. Eugene D. Genovese, "Marxian Interpretations of the Slave South," in Barton J. Bernstein, ed. *Towards a New Past,* (New York, 1968), 100, 112–13; *World the Slaveholders Made*, 118–244.

21. *World the Slaveholders Made*, 129.

22. Drew G. Faust, *A Sacred Circle* (Baltimore, 1977), 127.

23. Ibid., 130. For a primary account which shows that the planters were not prebourgeois or pre-capitalist, see Joseph G. Baldwin, *The Flush Times of Alabama and Mississippi* (New York, 1953), passim.

24. Genovese, *Roll, Jordan, Roll*, 3.

25. Lawrence W. Levine, *Black Culture and Black Consciousness* (New York, 1977), 5.

26. Three recent efforts to show how slavery changed through time are Herbert G. Gutman's *The Black Family in Slavery and Freedom 1750–1925*; Gerald W. Mullin, *Flight and Rebellion* (New York, 1972); Michael Mullin, ed., *American Negro Slavery* (New York, 1976).

27. Elizabeth Fox-Genovese and Eugene D. Genovese, "The Political Crisis of Social History: A Marxian Perspective," *Journal of Social History* 10 (1976), 219. For a corroboration of these ideas see E. P. Thompson's essay "Eighteenth-Century English Society: Class Struggle without Class?" *Social History* 3 (May 1978), 135–137.

28. Genovese, *Roll, Jordan, Roll*, 5.

29. Mullin, *American Negro Slavery*, 156–96. See also, Michael Wal-

lace, "Paternalism and Violence," in Philip P. Wiener and John Fisher, eds., *Violence and Aggression in the History of Ideas* (New Brunswick, N.J., 1974), 203–20. Wallace's essay contains some interesting comments about the use of paternalistic language. Genovese makes the mistake of adopting the language of his historical subjects. In doing this he implicitly endorses the planter's claim that their social system was superior to that of the industrial bourgeois of the North. One conclusion that can be drawn from this line of argument is that slavery was a benign institution. Genovese never argues this, but this is an interpretation that can be drawn from his method. See Genovese, *The World the Slaveholders Made*, 95–102, 165–244; and *Roll, Jordan, Roll*, 3–158. For a more systematic critique of Genovese on paternalism see James Oakes, *The Ruling Race* (New York, 1982), passim. See also Oakes most recent book, *Slavery And Freedom* (New York, 1990).

30. Quoted in Mullin, *American Negro Slavery*, 168.

31. *Plantation Life in the Florida Parishes of Louisiana 1836–1846 As Reflected in the Diary of Bennet H. Barrow*, Edwin Adams Davis, ed. (New York, 1943), 85–192, 202–376.

32. Ibid., 98.

33. Wish, *Ante-Bellum*, passim.

34. Mullin, *Flight and Rebellion*, 62–67.

35. Harriet Beecher Stowe, *Uncle Tom's Cabin, or Life among the Lowly* (1881; New York, 1962), passim.

36. *Slave Life in Georgia: A Narrative of the Life, Sufferings, and Escape of John Brown, A Fugitive Slave*, F.N. Boney, ed. (1855; Savannah, Ga., 1972); *Twelve Years a Slave: Narrative of Solomon Northup*, Sue Eakin and Joseph Logsdon, eds. (1853; Baton Rouge, 1968); *Austin Steward: Twenty-Two Years a Slave and Forty Years a Freeman*, Jane H. Pease and William H. Pease, eds. (1856; Reading, Pa., 1969).

37. Genovese, *Roll, Jordan, Roll*, preface, 16.

38. Ira Berlin, *Slaves without Masters* (New York, 1974); George Fredrickson, *The Black Image in the White Mind* (New York, 1971), chs. 1–6; Leon F. Litwack, *North of Slavery* (Chicago, 1961); James A. Rawley, *Race and Politics* (New York, 1969); William Stanton, *The Leopard's Spots* (Chicago, 1960).

39. Genovese, *Roll, Jordan, Roll*, 3.

40. Carl Degler makes these comments in *Perspectives and Irony in American Slavery*, Harry P. Owens, ed. (Jackson, Miss., 1976), 22.

41. See, for example, Berlin, *Slaves without Masters*; Carl Degler, *Neither Black nor White* (New York, 1971); Litwack, *North of Slavery.*

42. Owens, *Perspectives and Irony in American Slavery,* 22.

43. Quoted in William L. Barney, *The Road to Secession* (New York, 1972), 89.

44. Quoted in Degler, *The Other South,* 25.

45. Ronald G. Walters, *The Antislavery Appeal* (Baltimore, 1976), ch. 5.

46. Robert Blauner, *Racial Oppression in America* (New York, 1972), 145-46.

47. Hostility toward the Irish was a carryover from Europe. For the European history of this prejudice see Richard Ned Lebow, *White Britain and Black Ireland* (Philadelphia, 1976); L.P. Curtis, Jr., *Anglo-Saxon and Celts* (New York, 1968); *Apes and Angels* (Washington, D.C., 1971). In America a sense of this animus can be gained by reading the following: Ray Allen Billington, *The Protestant Crusade 1800-1860* (1938; Chicago, 1974); Oscar Handlin, *Boston's Immigrants* (Cambridge, Mass., 1921); Joel H. Silbey, ed., *The Transformation of American Politics 1840-1860* (Englewood Cliffs, N.J., 1967), 44.

48. Withrop Jordan, *White over Black* (Chapel Hill, N.C., 1968), see ch. 2., esp. pp. 91-98; and Edmund S. Morgan, *American Slavery American Freedom* (New York, 1975), ch. 15.

49. Helen T. Catterall, ed., *Judicial Cases Concerning American Slavery and the Negro,* 5 vols. (Washington, D.C., 1936), 5 (1859):257.

50. Ibid., 4 (1838):215.

51. Jordan, *White over Black,* 80, 81, 97; Stampp, *The Peculiar Institution,* 22-23.

52. Genovese, *Roll, Jordan, Roll,* 4-5.

53. Vincent Harding, "Religion and Resistance among Antebellum Negroes, 1800-1860," in August Meier and Elliott Rudwick, eds., *The Making of Black America,* 2 vols. (New York, 1969), 1:179-97; Gayraud S. Wilmore, *Black Religion and Black Radicalism* (New York, 1973), ch. 1-3.

54. Genovese, *Roll, Jordan, Roll,* 6.

55. Ibid., 183, 209-55.

56. Ibid., 182.

57. Ibid., 232-80. See also, Albert J. Raboteau, "The Invisible Institution: The Origins and Conditions of Black Religion before Eman-

cipation," (Ph.D. diss., Yale University, 1975), 127-78; Milton C. Sernett, *Black Religion and American Evangelicalism* (Metuchen, N.J., 1975), ch. 4.

58. Genovese, *Roll, Jordan, Roll*, 232-79. See also Levine, *Black Culture and Black Consciousness*, 5-80.

59. Genovese, *Roll, Jordan, Roll*, 281. See also Genovese's comments on this subject in his famous essay the "Legacy of Slavery and Roots of Black Nationalism," *Studies on the Left* 6 (1966), 4-5. This essay has been revised and appears in *In Red and Black*, 127-57.

60. Genovese and Genovese, "The Political Crisis of Social History: A Marxian Perspective," 219.

61. *Roll, Jordan, Roll*, 272-79.

62. I want to thank Professor John Jentz for letting me see a pre-publication copy of his article "A Note on Genovese's Account of the Slaves' Religion," *Civil War History* 23 (June 1977), 161-69. This paper explains Genovese's curious interpretation of the doctrine of original sin and millennialism.

63. Genovese, *Roll, Jordan, Roll*, 211-12, 245-47.

64. Ibid., 209-11.

65. Ibid., 212.

66. Ibid., 272-74, 276.

67. Ibid., 276.

68. Richard Allen, *The Life Experience and Gospel Labors of the Rt. Rev. Richard Allen* (Nashville, Tenn., 18??); *An Autobiography of the Reverend Josiah Henson*, Robin Winks, ed. (1881; Reading, Pa., 1969), 25; *The Great Slave Narratives*, Arna Bontemps, ed. (1849; Boston, 1969), 243; William H. Heard, *From Slavery to the Bishopric* (1924; New York, 1969), 63-64.

69. Allen, *The Life Experiences*, 7.

70. Clifton H. Johnson, ed., *God Struck Me Dead* (Boston, 1969), see p. 9 of the introduction.

71. Genovese, *Roll, Jordan, Roll*, 272.

72. Quoted in Phillips, *American Negro Slavery*, 294-95.

73. Martin Marty makes these remarks in the foreword of Sernett, *Black Religion and American Evangelicalism*, 15.

74. Genovese, *Roll, Jordan, Roll*, 587-97.

75. Ibid., 638-48.

76. Boggs, *Gramsci's Marxism*, 39-40.

77. Camett, Antonio Gramsci, 204; Hoare and Smith, *Selections from the Prison Notebooks*, 12.

78. Genovese, *Roll, Jordan, Roll*, 254–55.

79. Degler, *Place over Time*, 73–83; James A. Henretta, "Social History as Lived and Written," *American Historical Review* 84 (Dec. 1975), 1332. See also Paul Escott's discussion of Genovese's hegemonic framework in *Slavery Remembered* (Chapel Hill, N.C., 1979), ch. 1.

80. I should like to thank Professors Frank Tipton, Jr., Ronald Walters, and Kenneth Stampp for reading earlier drafts of this article.

Chapter 4
Black Reconstruction in America:
The Challenge of W.E.B. DuBois

1. Robert Penn Warren, *The Legacy of the Civil War* (New York, 1961), 3.

2. John W. Burgess, *Reconstruction and the Constitution, 1866–1876* (New York, 1902); William Archibald Dunning, *Reconstruction, Political and Economic* (New York, 1907); Thomas Nelson Page, "The Southern People during Reconstruction," *The Atlantic Monthly* 88 (September 1901); Woodrow Wilson, "The Reconstruction of the Southern States," *The Atlantic Monthly* 87 (January 1901). Two books that depart from this tradition are John Hope Franklin, *Reconstruction: After the Civil War* (Chicago, 1961), and Kenneth M. Stampp, *The Era of Reconstruction 1865–1877* (New York, 1965). See also Bernard Weisberger, "The Dark and Bloody Ground of Reconstruction Historiography," *Journal of Southern History* 25, no. 2 (Nov. 1959), 427–47.

3. James Shepherd Pike, *The Prostrate State: South Carolina under Negro Government*, Robert F. Durden, ed. (1873; New York, 1968); xlii.

4. Stampp, *The Era of Reconstruction, 1865–1877*, ch. 1.

5. Pike, *The Prostrate State*, 50.

6. Ibid., 66.

7. Ibid., 67–68.

8. Quoted in William Gillette, *Retreat from Reconstruction, 1869–1879* (Baton Rouge, 1979), 217.

9. James Ford Rhodes, *History of the United States, Vol. VII, 1872–1877* (New York, 1906), 171.

10. Burgess, *Reconstruction and the Constitution*, 249, 252, 296.

11. Dunning, *Reconstruction Politics and Economics*, passim; Walter

L. Flemming, *The Sequel of Appomattox* (New Haven, Conn., 1919); Woodrow Wilson, *A History of the American People*, vol. 5 (New York, 1903).

12. Quoted in Leslie Fiedler, *What Was Literature?* (New York, 1982), 180.

13. Michael Rogin, "The Sword Became a Flashing Vision: D.W. Griffith's *The Birth of a Nation*," *Representations* 9 (Winter 1985), 150–95.

14. Richard Slotkin, *The Fatal Environment* (New York, 1985), 16.

15. Ulrich Bonnell Phillips, *Life and Labor in the Old South*, 194–217, in Allen Weinstein and Frank Otto Gatell, eds., *American Negro Slavery*, 2nd ed. (New York: Oxford University Press, 1973), 68.

16. Quoted in Clarence E. Walker, "The American Negro as Historical Outsider, 1836–1935," *The Canadian Review of American Studies* 17 (Summer 1986), 146.

17. George Wilhelm Friedrich Hegel, *The Philosophy of History* (1899; New York, 1956), 98.

18. Quoted in Harold R. Isaacs, "Pan-Africanism as Romantic Racism," in Rayford W. Logan, ed., *W.E.B. DuBois: A Profile* (New York, 1971), 215.

19. W.E.B. DuBois, *Dusk of Dawn* (1940; New York, 1968), 139. DuBois would have eschewed the idea that because something was socially constructed it could be easily deconstructed. This point escapes Thomas C. Holt in his essay "The Political Uses of Alienation: W.E.B. DuBois on Politics, Race, and Culture, 1903–1940," in *American Quarterly* 42 (June 1990), 304.

20. Eric Foner, *Nothing but Freedom* (Baton Rouge, 1983); Ferrucio Gambino, "W.E.B. DuBois and the Proletariat in Black Reconstruction," in Dirk Hoerder, ed., *American Labor and Immigration History, 1877–1920s* (Urbana, Ill., 1983), 43–60; Paul Richards, "W.E.B. DuBois and American Social History: The Evolution of a Marxist," *Radical History* 4 (1970), 37–65; Kenneth M. Stampp, *The Era of Reconstruction*, ch. 1; T. Harry Williams, "An Analysis of Some Reconstruction Attitudes," *Journal of Southern History* 17, (November 1946), 469–86.

21. DuBois, *Dusk of Dawn*, 205.

22. W.E.B. DuBois, "Why the Socialist Flag Is Red," *The Horizon* 3 (February 1908), 8.

23. W.E.B. DuBois, *The Autobiography of W.E.B. DuBois* (New York 1968), 289.

24. W.E.B. DuBois, "Socialism and the Negro Problem," *The New Review* 1 (February 1913), 139.

25. Ibid., 138.

26. Ibid., 139.

27. Ibid., 7–8.

28. W.E.B. DuBois, "Marxism and the Negro Problem," *Crisis* 40 (May 1933), 104.

29. Ibid.

30. Ibid.

31. W.E.B. DuBois, "Karl Marx and the Negro," *Crisis* 40 (March 1933), 6.

32. Quoted in William M. Tuttle, ed., *W.E.B. DuBois* (Englewood Cliffs, N.J., 1973), 85.

33. Quoted in ibid.

34. Charles Crowe, "The Emergence of Progressive History," *Journal of the History of Ideas* 31 (January–March 1966), 113. See also Richard Hofstadter, *The Progressive Historians* (New York, 1968).

35. Crowe, "The Emergence of Progressive History," 112.

36. Quoted in John Barker, *The Super Historians* (New York, 1982), 240.

37. DuBois, *Dusk of Dawn*, 139.

38. Ibid., 5, 115.

39. Ibid., 131–33.

40. DuBois, *The Souls of Black Folk*, 22.

41. DuBois, *Black Reconstruction* (New York, 1935). See "To the Reader."

42. Weisberger, "The Dark and Bloody Ground of Reconstruction Historiography," 427–47.

43. Burgess, *Reconstruction and the Constitution*, 133.

44. DuBois, "Reconstruction and Its Benefits," *The American Historical Review* 15 (July 1910), 781–99.

45. See, for example, Dunning, *Reconstruction, Political and Economic*.

46. DuBois, *Dusk of Dawn*, 318–19.

47. DuBois, *Black Reconstruction*, 708.

48. Ibid., chs. 1 and 2.

49. Peter Singer, *Marx* (New York, 1980), 21.

50. DuBois, *Black Reconstruction*, ch. 4.

51. Ibid., 358.

52. Ibid., 357–58. See also, for this tension, pages 22, 25, 27, 30, 39, 80, 81, 367.

53. Aileen S. Kraditor, *The Radical Persuasion, 1890–1917* (Baton Rouge, 1981), 163.

54. Ibid., 163.

55. DuBois, *Black Reconstruction*, chs. 10 and 11.

56. Vernon Lane Wharton, *The Negro in Mississippi, 1865–1890* (1947; New York, 1965), 59.

57. Elizabeth Ware Pearson, ed., *Letters from Port Royal* (1906; New York, 1969), 37–39. The freedman Limus is not an exception, as this quote indicates. Limus and his peers were part of a tradition of black American entrepreneurship that dates back to the eighteenth century. Economic activity in the nineteenth century, black spokesmen thought, would solve the race problem by showing that American Negroes possessed initiative and were not slothful and lazy. In both the black church and the northern pre-Civil War free Negro conventions, a great emphasis was placed on the marketplace as an agent of Negro equality. In the antebellum South a minority of the free Negroes and slaves participated in the marketplace. Eric Foner errs when he writes: "The slave's standard of consumption, and his experience with the marketplace, was, of necessity, very limited. The logic of ever-greater effort to meet ever-expanding needs (what capitalist society calls "ambition") had no meaning for him." Foner mistakenly equates a hostility to harsh labor with an antipathy to the marketplace. He also elides the historic consumerist propensity of black American culture. Stated another way, Foner's argument ignores the fact that after the Civil War some of the freedmen ran off to the cities of the South in search of work. In the cities these ex-slaves had to bargain for work and wages. Where did their knowledge of these processes come from? It also fails to account for the freedmen's desire for consumer goods after the war. Gerald D. Jaynes, Lawrence Powell, Roger L. Ransome and Richard Sutch's studies of emancipated slaves all indicate that there was a desire among the freedmen for goods produced outside the household. Furthermore, before the Civil War some slaves purchased themselves and their loved ones. This activity required some knowledge on the part of the slaves of market forces. Finally, sources as diverse as *Frederick Douglass's Narrative and Autobiography* and Richard C. Wade's *Slavery in the Cities* show that the practice of slave hiring was undermined by the slaves' working deals with their employers that undermined their masters' authority. The quote is from Eric Foner, *Politics and Ideology*

in the Age of the Civil War (New York, 1980), 106, see also 98–101, and Foner, *Reconstruction: America's Unfinished Revolution, 1863–1877,* 155–70. The discussion of blacks and the marketplace is based on my reading of the following works: Howard H. Bell, ed., *Minutes of the Proceedings of the National Negro Convention, 1830–1864* (New York, 1969), passim; see also Clarence E. Walker, *A Rock in a Weary Land,* ch. 1. The following studies show how the market affected the thought and aspirations of free Negroes and slaves: Ira Berlin, *Slaves without Masters* (New York, 1974); Luther P. Jackson, *Free Negro Labor and Property Holding in Virginia, 1830–1860* (1942; New York, 1968); Michael P. Johnson and James L. Roark, *Black Masters* (New York, 1984). See also these autobiographies: *Free Man of Color: The Autobiography of Willis Hodges,* Willard B. Gatewood, Jr., ed. (1890s; Knoxville, Tenn., 1982); *Slave and Freeman: The Autobiography of George L. Knox* (1894–95; Lexington, Ky., 1979); *North Into Freedom: The Autobiography of John Malvin, Free Negro, 1795–1880,* Allen Peskin, ed. (1879; Cleveland, Ohio, 1966); Austin Steward, *Twenty-Two Years a Slave and Forty Years a Freeman* (1857; Reading, Pa., 1969); *From Tennessee Slave to St. Louis Entrepreneur: The Autobiography of James Thomas,* Loren Schweninger, ed. (1903–1904; Colombia, Mo., 1984). Arguments and evidence indicating Foner overstated his case may be found in Gerald D. Jaynes, *Branches without Roots* (New York, 1986), 184; Lawrence D. Powell, *New Masters* (New Haven, Conn., 1980), 87–89; and Roger L. Ransome and Richard Sutch, *One Kind of Freedom* (Cambridge, Mass., 1977) passim.

Chapter 5
The American Negro as Historical Outsider, 1836–1935

This chapter was published previously as an article in the *"Canadian Review of American Studies* 17, no. 2 (Summer 1986). It is used by permission.

1. George Fredrickson, *White Supremacy* (New York, 1981), xi–xii.
2. Quoted in Benjamin Quarles, "Black History's Antebellum Origins," *The Proceedings of the American Antiquarian Society* 89, no. 1 (April 1979), 89. After I completed this essay two important books on black history were published. See Darlene Clark Hine, *The State of Afro-American History: Past, Present, and Future* (Baton Rouge, 1986); Au-

gust Meier and Elliott Rudwick, *Black History and the Historical Profession, 1915–1980* (Urbana, Ill., 1985).

3. William Wells Brown, *The Black Man, His Antecedents, His Genius, and His Achievements* (Boston, 1856), and *The Rising Son; Or, The Antecedents and Advancement of the Colored Race* (Boston, 1874); Martin Robinson Delany, *The Condition, Elevation, Emigration and Destiny of the Colored People of the United States* (Philadelphia, 1852). I have included this last book in my list of the histories although most students of American black history tend to think of *The Condition* as a black nationalist tract. It is this and more, for the heart of the book, chapters 8–15, is a collection of historical sketches which reveal, to quote Delany the "capacity of Colored men and women as citizen members of the community." James Theodore Holly, "A Vindication of the Capacity of the Negro Race for Self-Government and Civilized Progress," in Howard H. Bell, ed., *Black Separation* (Ann Arbor, Mich., 1970), 21–66; Robert Benjamin Lewis, *Light and Truth; Collected from the Bible and Ancient and Modern History; Containing the Universal History of the Colored and the Indian Race, from the Creation of the World to the Present Time* (1836; Portland, Maine, 1844); William Cooper Nell, *The Colored Patriots of the American Revolution* (Boston, 1855); James W. C. Pennington, *A Textbook of the Origin and History of the Colored People* (Hartford, Conn., 1841); George Washington Williams, *History of the Negro Race in America 1619–1880* (1883; New York, 1968); Joseph T. Wilson, *The Black Phalanx: A History of the Negro Soldiers of the United States in the Wars of 1775–1812, 1861–1865* (Hartford, Conn., 1890).

4. In *The Life Labors of the Rt. Rev. Richard Allen* (Nashville, Tenn., n.d.), 31–48.

5. Brown, *Rising Sun*, 39, and *Black Man*, 32–33; Lewis, *Light and Truth*, passim; Pennington, *A Textbook*, 47–48; Williams, *History of the Negro Race*, 1: 110.

6. See Fredrickson, *The Black Image in the White Mind* (New York, 1971), 71–96; and William Stanton, *The Leopard's Spots* (Chicago, 1960), passim.

7. Quoted in Quarles, "Antebellum Origins," 91.

8. Howard Dodson, "Needed: A New Perspective on Black History," *Humanities* 2, no. 1 (Feb. 1981), 1–2.

9. Clarence Walker, *A Rock in a Weary Land: The African Methodist Episcopal Church during the Civil War and Reconstruction* (Baton Rouge, 1982), ch. 1.

10. Holly, "A Vindication," passim. See also the orations on the abolition of the slave trade in Dorothy Porter, ed. *Early Negro Writing, 1760–1837*, (Boston, 1971), 334–404.

11. *Savannah Colored American*, 13 Jan. 1866.

12. Bishop L. H. Holsey, *Autobiography, Sermons, Addresses, and Essays* (Atlanta, 1898), 242–43; Frederick Douglass, *My Bondage and My Freedom* (1855; New York, 1968), 90; Williams, *History of the Negro Race*, 1:113–14.

13. Leonard Sweet, *Black Historians: A Critique* (New York, 1971), 3–13, 42.

14. Maria W. Stewart, "An Address Delivered at the African Masonic Hall Boston February 27, 1833," in Porter, 130–31.

15. Earl Thorpe, *Black Historians: A Critique* (New York, 1971), 3–13, 42.

16. Brown, *Rising Son*, ch. 50. Williams, *History*, 1: ch. 29; 2: 23. See also these autobiographies: *Free Man of Color: The Autobiography of Willis Hodges*, Willard B. Gatewood, Jr., ed. (1890s; Knoxville, 1982); *Slave and Freeman: The Autobiography of George L. Knox* (1894–95; Lexington, Ky., 1979); *North into Freedom: The Autobiography of John Malvin, Free Negro, 1795–1880*, Allen Peskin, ed. (1879; Cleveland, 1966); Austin Steward, *Twenty-Two Years a Slave and Forty Years a Freeman* (1857; Reading, Pa., 1969); *From Tennessee Slave to St. Louis Entrepreneur: The Autobiography of James Thomas*, Loren Schweninger, ed. (1903–1904; Columbia, Mo., 1984).

17. William Wells Brown, *The Negro in the American Rebellion* (Boston, 1867); Nell, *Colored Patriots*; George Washington Williams, *A History of the Negro Troops in the War of the Rebellion, 1861–1865* (New York, 1888); Wilson, *Black Phalanx*.

18. Nell, *Colored Patriots*, 9, 378; Brown, *Negro in the American Rebellion*, chs. 2, 5, 7.

19. Thomas B. Macaulay, "History and Literature," in Franz Stern, ed., *The Varieties of History* (New York, 1972), 78.

20. Antonio Gramsci, *Selections from the Prison Notebooks*, ed. and trans. Quintin Hoare and Geoffrey Nowell Smith (New York, 1978), 324–25.

21. William J. Simmons, *Men of Mark* (1887; Chicago, 1970).

22. Jacob Katz, *Out of the Ghetto: The Social Background of Jewish Emancipation 1770–1870* (New York, 1978).

23. *From Persecution to Destruction: Anti-Semitism, 1700–1933* (Cambridge, Mass., 1980), 103, 226.

24. "Four Letters by Sidney," *The Colored American*, 13 March 1841, in Sterling Stuckey, ed. *The Ideological Origins of Black Nationalism* (Boston, 1972), 161. See also 145.

25. Steven E. Aschheim, *Brothers and Strangers: The East European Jews in German and German Jewish Consciousness, 1800–1923* (Madison, Wis., 1982); Michael R. Marrus, *The Politics of Assimilation* (Oxford, Eng., 1971); William O. McCagg, Jr., *Jewish Nobles and Geniuses in Modern Hungary* (Boulder, Colo., 1972).

26. *Independent Monitor*, 23 Feb. 1869, quoted in Allen W. Trelease, *White Terror* (New York, 1972), 254.

27. For the specifics of Williams's career see the following articles and book by John Hope Franklin, "George Washington Williams, Historian," *Journal of Negro History* 31 (Jan. 1946), 60–90; "George Washington Williams and the Beginning of Afro-American Historiography," *Critical Inquiry* 4 (Summer 1978), 756–72; "Afro-American Biography: The Case of George Washington Williams," *Proceedings of the American Philosophical Society* 123 (April 1979), 160–63; "Stalking George Washington Williams," *National Humanities Center Newsletter* 3 (Winter 1981–82), 24–29; "George Washington Williams: The Massachusetts Years" (Worcester, Mass., reprinted from *The Proceedings of the American Antiquarian Society* 92, no. 2 (Oct. 1982), 243–63, *George Washington Williams* (Chicago, 1985).

28. See Alexander Crummell, "The Relations and Duties of Free Colored Men in America to Africa," in Howard Brotz, ed., *Negro Social and Political Thought, 1850–1920* (New York, 1966), 171–80.

29. August Meier, *Negro Thought in America 1880–1915* (Ann Arbor, Mich., 1963), 26–41.

30. Quoted in William Appleman Williams, *The Contours of American History* (Cleveland, Ohio, 1961), 323.

31. W.E.B. DuBois, *Dusk of Dawn* (1940; New York, 1968), 29.

32. Thomas F. Gossett, *Race: The History of an Idea in America* (New York, 1965); John Higham, *Strangers in the Land* (New Brunswick, N.J., 1955), 131–57.

33. Higham, *Strangers*, 135.

34. Jurgen Herbst, *The German Historical School in American Scholarship* (Ithaca, N.Y., 1965), 116, 118. See also, Edward N. Saveth, "Race and Nationalism in American Historiography: The Late Nineteenth Century," *Political Science Quarterly* 54 (Sept. 1939), 421–41.

35. Quoted in Herbst, *German Historical School*, 123.

36. Woodrow Wilson, "The Reconstruction of the Southern States," *The Atlantic Monthly* 87 (Jan. 1901), 6.

37. John R. Commons, *Races and Immigrants in America* (New York, 1907), 403.

38. See, for example, the articles written by John R. Lynch on his correspondence with James Ford Rhodes: "Some Historical Errors of James Ford Rhodes," *The Journal of Negro History* 2 (Oct. 1917), 345–68; "More about the Historical Errors of James F. Rhodes," *Journal of Negro History* 3 (April 1918), 139–57.

39. Frederick Bancroft, *The Negro in Politics* (New York, 1885), 15; Phillip A. Bruce, *The Plantation Negro as a Freeman* (1889; Williamstown, N.Y., 1970). See also John W. Burgess, *Reconstruction and the Constitution 1866–1876* (New York, 1902), 252, 263, 64.

40. Kenneth Milton Stampp, "The Tragic Legend of Reconstruction," in *The Era of Reconstruction 1865–1877* (New York, 1965), 3–23; Bernard Weisberger, "The Dark and Bloody Ground of Reconstruction Historiography," *Journal of Southern History* 25, no. 4 (Nov. 1959), 422–47.

41. W.E.B. DuBois, *The Autobiography of W.E.B. DuBois* (New York, 1968), 75.

42. For Woodson's life and career, see Jacqueline Anne Goggin, "Carter G. Woodson and the Movement to Promote Black History" (Ph.D. diss., University of Rochester, 1983); and Patricia Watkins Romero, "Carter G. Woodson: A Biography" (Ph.D. diss., Ohio State University, 1971).

43. Meier, *Negro Thought*, 136, 262; Goggin, "Carter G. Woodson," ch. 1.

44. See, for example, Woodson, *History of the Negro Church* (1921; Washington, D.C., 1972).

45. See, for example, Woodson, *The Mind of the Negro as Reflected in Letters Written during the Crisis 1800–1860* (1926; New York, 1969).

46. Woodson, "Negro Life and History in Our Schools," *Journal of Negro History* 4 (July 1919), 274–75, 277.

47. Woodson, "Negro History Week," *Journal of Negro History* 11 (April 1926), 240–41.

48. Woodson, "Negro Life and History," 279.

49. DuBois, "A Portrait of Carter G. Woodson," *Masses and Mainstream* 3 (June 1950), 19–25.

50. DuBois, *Dusk of Dawn*, 25–49, 29, 98.

51. Ibid., 98.

52. See, for example, DuBois, *The Philadelphia Negro* (1899; New York, 1967).

53. DuBois, *Dusk of Dawn*, 5, 32, 34, 50, 51, 58, 60, 61.

54. DuBois, "The Conservation of Races," in the *American Negro Academy Occasional Papers* (1897; New York, 1969), 2:5-15; *The Souls of Black Folk* (1903; Greenwich, Conn., 1961).

55. Allison Davis, "The Intellectual as Leader: The Lonely Warrior, W.E.B. DuBois," in *Leadership, Love and Aggression* (New York, 1983), 130.

56. DuBois, "Reconstruction and Its Benefits," *American Historical Review* 15 (1910), 781-99.

57. See William A. Dunning, *Reconstruction, Political and Economic 1865-1877* (1907; New York, 1962).

58. DuBois, *Black Reconstruction* (New York, 1935), 708.

59. DuBois, *The Suppression of the African Slave Trade to the United States, 1638-1870* (1898; New York, 1965), 327-29.

60. See Barbara J. Fields, "Ideology and Race in American History," in J. Morgan Kousser and James M. McPherson, eds., *Region, Race and Reconstruction: Essays in Honor of C. Vann Woodward* (New York, 1982), 143-78; Armistead Robinson, "Beyond the Realm of Social Consensus: New Meanings of Reconstruction for American History," *The Journal of American History* 68 (Sept. 1981), 276-97.

61. L.D. Reddick, "A New Interpretation for Negro History," *Journal of Negro History* 22 (Jan. 1937), 17-28.

Bibliographic Essay

A full list of the citations for this book may be found in the footnotes. This brief essay is intended to give my readers some idea of the articles and books that I think were important in shaping my arguments in these articles.

Chapter 1

Chapter 1 of this collection deals with the problem of using class as the major prescriptor for nineteenth-century American history. Marxist and neo-Marxist readers of this essay will accuse me of being an essentialist. Although I may seem to accord race an unchanging place in my analysis, I mean only to give race the relative autonomy it deserves in any serious analysis of nineteenth-century American history. I do this because the work criticized in this piece either treats race as class or denies its importance by arguing it is only a social construct. I do not deny that race is a social construct, but the argument cannot end by just noting this fact. Since everything is socially constructed what are historians telling us when they say race is too? I think they are declaring that because race is a creation of the mind it can be easily deconstructed. This line of argument is naive and ahistorical. For example, femaleness is also a socially constructed category and if the concept were abolished tomorrow some women would indubitably continue to be female. The working class is also conceptualized in a similar fashion; until recently some American historians have tried to ignore or deny its importance in United States history. This omission in historical analysis has not caused the working class to disappear. The point I am making here is that ideas about gender, race, religion, or the working class persist over and through time. The social world in which these categories of analysis exist may change but the phenomena persist. The following works have helped me to arrive at the conclusion that race has a relative autonomy and cannot be treated as a form of class in the nineteenth century: Michael Banton, *Racial Theories* (Cambridge, Mass., 1989); Sander L. Gilman, *Difference and Pathology* (Ithaca, N.Y., 1985); Frank Parkin, *Marxism And Class Theory: A Bourgeois Critique* (New York, 1979); Judith Stacey, *Patriarchy and Socialist Revolution In China* (Berkeley, Calif., 1983); and Keith Thomas, *Religion and the Decline of Magic* (Harmonsworth, Eng., 1971).

Chapter 2

Twenty three years ago as a graduate student at the University of California, Berkeley, I heard Professor Leon F. Litwack deliver a lecture on Marcus Garvey. During the lecture Professor Litwack quoted Garvey as saying ". . . his Fascism preceded that of Mussolini and Hitler." This statement made me think there was more to Garvey than the standard interpretation of his life and career revealed. Subsequent reading in the literature of Garveyism convinced me that Garveyism had a racist and reactionary side. For example, in a 1937 interview, Joel A. Rogers reports that Garvey claimed:

> "We were the first Fascists," [Garvey] said, "when we had 100,000 disciplined men, and were training children, Mussolini was still an unknown. Mussolini copied our Fascism."

Later on Garvey observed that the "UNIA was before Mussolini and Hitler ever were heard of. Mussolini and Hitler copied the program of the UNIA — aggressive nationalism for the black man in Africa." Both of these quotations are in Robert Hill and Barbara Bair, eds., *Marcus Garvey Life and Lessons* (Berkeley, Calif., 1987), Introduction, lviii. My analysis of Garvey has been shaped by reading Boyd C. James's "Primitives on the Move: Some Historical Articulations of Garvey and Garveyism, 1887–1927" (Ph.D. dissertation, University of California, Los Angeles, 1982). This is a brilliant dissertation and should be published as a book. Amy Jacques Garvey, *Garvey and Garveyism* (Kingston, Jamaica, 1963) is an insightful text for understanding the cultural symbols of Garveyism. In dealing with Garveyism American historians have been very parochial in their explanation of this manifestation of black nationalism. I think work in comparative nationalism will broaden our understanding of Garveyism. The following works on Zionism and European right-wing movements have been particularly useful: Shlomo Avineri, *The Making of Modern Zionism* (New York, 1981), 88–100, 159–86, Jacques Kornberg, "Theodore Herzl: A Re-evaluation," *Journal of Modern History* 52 (June 1980), 226–52; Peter Lowenberg, *Decoding the Past* (New York, 1983), 101–35; Juan G. Linz, "Some Notes Toward a Comparative Study of Fascism in Sociological Historical Perspective (Berkeley, Calif., 1978), 9, 12–13; and Dennis Mack Smith, *Mussolini* (New York, 1982).

Chapter 3

Since I wrote this essay I have not changed my ideas about this fine book. If I were to rewrite this article I would expand the section of the paper dealing with slave religion.

Chapters 4 and 5

These two chapters will appear in revised form in my study of black history, *Defenders of the Race*. In working on this monograph I have benefited from some recent articles and books dealing with the historiography of black history. See Darlene Clark Hine, ed., *The State of Afro-American History* (Baton Rouge, 1986); Nathan I. Huggins, "Afro-American History: Myths, Heroes, Reality," in Nathan Huggins, Martin Kilson, Daniel Fox, eds., *Key Issues in the Afro-American-Experience*, I (New York, 1971), 5–19; John B. Kirby, "An Uncertain Context, America and Black Americans in the Twentieth Century," *Journal of Southern History* 46 (November 1980), 571–86; Orlando Patterson, "Rethinking Black History," *Harvard Educational Review* 41 (August 1971), 297–315; Benjamin Quarles, *Black History's Antebellum Origins*, (Worcester, Mass., 1979); August Meier and Elliott Rudwick, *Black History and the Historical Profession 1915–1980* (Urbana, Ill., 1986).

Index